Praise for *Faithful Finance*

Money stirs up a mixed bag of emotions—a spectrum of hopes and fears—especially when we think about our futures. Emily Stroud knows how to navigate what you're feeling and thinking about money and empowers you to maximize your resources, give generously, and save big. I highly recommend *Faithful Finance* for anyone who wants to live the truly abundant life.

—Margaret Feinberg, author
of *Fight Back with Joy*

Faithful Finance offers practical advice, rooted in the Bible, for those who seek to honor God with their money. Emily G. Stroud presents clear, motivational strategies that readers will find encouraging and doable. She is an expert in financial management, she is a lover of God's Word, she is a dedicated wife and mother, and she is my sister. Emily has offered me helpful financial guidance and she lives what she teaches. This book helps connect the dots for those seeking to live on a budget as they live for Jesus. Read *Faithful Finance* for your own family and then share it with another family. You will all be blessed.

—Trey Graham, senior pastor of First Melissa

If you've ever felt overwhelmed or confused when it comes to managing money, stop everything and read this book immediately! Without over-complicating matters or boring you, Emily G. Stroud maps out a clear path for your finances—careful to always point readers toward what matters most. You'll love her inspiring spirit and deep insight. Begin your journey toward *Faithful Finance* today!

—Cherie Lowe, author of *Slaying the Debt Dragon*

This is a must-read for anyone willing to admit the only knowledge they have about money is how to spend it, but also wants some to spend in the future. Emily meets the reader where they are and tenderly guides them to a comprehensive plan to make sure everyone is cared for, from aging grandparents to future grandchildren. Her compassionate heart shines through in every chapter as she desires for the reader to enjoy a better life by being more informed and intentional with their resources. She does this by defining financial terms in easy-to-understand language and by recommending practical tips that can be immediately applied. Her approach, illustrated by the many testimonies in the book, is undergirded with Scripture and the constant reminder to pray. This is the one book I wish I had read when I received my first paycheck, and I will recommend it to anyone who frets over their finances.

–Dr. Cody McQueen, teaching pastor at Christ Chapel Bible Church, Fort Worth, Texas

Talking about finance and budgets can often seem like dry, daunting topics. However, Emily G. Stroud's book, *Faithful Finance*, makes them anything but boring. She uses fresh, fun, and fulfilling insights for simply mastering your money—rather than the other way around.

Emily is a self-employed financial advisor. However, her number one priority is being a wife and mother. *Faithful Finance* draws its fruitful and wise methods from Emily's two decades of experience as a Chartered Financial Analyst, as well as her personal experience with her own family. Most important, Emily utilizes an accurate reading of Scripture, which is extremely important in this day and age. I want you to know that Emily is the real deal. What you see is what you get. Her gift for making finances simple, sensible, and clear has helped me tremendously; I know she can do the same for you. Emily believes that the right approach can make managing your finances enjoyable, satisfying, and quickly rewarding. If enjoyable, satisfying, and quickly rewarding finances sounds good to you, all you need is this book: *Faithful Finance*.

–Mr. King Hoover, founder of Transforming Athletics

FAITHFUL
FINANCE

**10
SECRETS**
TO MOVE FROM
**FEARFUL
INSECURITY**
TO **CONFIDENT
CONTROL**

FAITHFUL
FINANCE

EMILY G. STROUD,
MBA, CFA

ZONDERVAN

Faithful Finance
Copyright © 2015, 2018 by Emily G. Stroud

Requests for information should be addressed to:
Zondervan, *3900 Sparks Dr. SE, Grand Rapids, Michigan 49546*

ISBN 978-0-310-34978-5 (hardcover)

ISBN 978-0-310-35159-7 (audio)

ISBN 978-0-310-35055-2 (ebook)

Scripture quotations are taken from the Holy Bible, New International Version®, NIV®. Copyright © 1973, 1978, 1984, 2011 by Biblica, Inc.® Used by permission of Zondervan. All rights reserved worldwide. www.Zondervan.com. The "NIV" and "New International Version" are trademarks registered in the United States Patent and Trademark Office by Biblica, Inc.®

Any Internet addresses (websites, blogs, etc.) and telephone numbers in this book are offered as a resource. They are not intended in any way to be or imply an endorsement by Zondervan, nor does Zondervan vouch for the content of these sites and numbers for the life of this book.

Some names and identifying details have been changed to protect the privacy of individuals mentioned in this work.

Author is represented by the literary agency of The Fedd Agency, Inc., P. O. Box 341973, Austin, Texas 78734.

Emily G. Stroud is a Registered Representative. Securities offered through Cambridge Investment Research, Inc., a Broker/Dealer, Member FINRA/SIPC. Investment Advisor Representative Cambridge Investment Research Advisors, Inc., a Registered Investment Advisor. Cambridge and Emily G. Stroud, LLC are not affiliated.

Art direction: Gradient
Interior design: Denise Froehlich

First printing November 2017 / Printed in the United States of America

To God and to all of those who
try to be faithful to him—
even with their money.

Contents

10. Proper Estate Planning Is a Great Legacy

Foreword

I've sailed across the Pacific twice. The first time, a couple friends and I volunteered to sail a guy's boat from Hawaii to San Francisco. We knew less than nothing about how to cross an ocean, but we figured if we kept sailing east for long enough, we'd hit either Seattle or Cabo. What could possibly go wrong? The answer is–plenty. We sailed right into a huge storm and broke the mast and a great deal of the rest of the boat. We limped into the San Francisco Bay weeks later in pretty bad shape. This isn't unlike the way some of us have managed our finances. We get a job, deposit a few paychecks, make a few purchases, point in a direction, and figure we'll make it to shore. Sometimes we do, and other times we don't.

The second time I crossed the Pacific, a few of us bought a cheap boat and entered the Transpac race, a sailboat race held every other year. The starting line is at Long Beach, California, and the finish line is in Oahu, Hawaii. With one trip filled with mistakes under our belts, we set out thinking this time things would turn out a little better. The rules of the Transpac race prohibit the use of any electronics or tools, such as a global positioning system for navigation. Instead, each boat needs to steer by the stars. It sounded easy enough, particularly because we had the navigator from a Navy destroyer on our crew. Shortly before the race however, the Navy changed his orders, and I became the navigator. While I had learned a few things about sailing, I knew nothing about navigation. We didn't wreck the boat like we did on the first trip, but we almost missed the entire Hawaiian island chain. Here's why: we needed someone who could navigate better than me.

Emily is a friend of mine, and she has written an excellent book. *Faithful Finance* isn't just a book about money; it's an invitation to begin learning how to navigate your finances. You won't learn a thing about how to get across an ocean, but you will learn more than a few things about how to get to where you want to go with your finances. But she's not going to do all of the work for you. In fact, the most important part of the journey you're setting out on will require you to do a little steering of your own.

You'll need to figure out where you want to end up. Emily is a terrific navigator, but you're the captain when it comes to picking your goals.

You're setting out on a terrific adventure. Raise your sails. Lift the anchor. Pick your direction with a navigator you can trust. Then come up with a financial direction and be sure to stay the course. I hope you enjoy *Faithful Finance* as much as I have.

-Bob Goff

Acknowledgments

Thanks to my father. You taught me how to love God, serve others, and be an entrepreneur. Thank you for teaching me that I can persevere and overcome many challenges as long as God is the anchor of my life. You have always been my biggest cheerleader. I love that you and Mom now call Forth Worth your home.

Thanks to my mother. You taught me the power of prayer and how to be a godly wife and mother. You have been the picture of grace during challenging health situations. I love you fiercely.

Thanks to my husband. You are my best friend, my encourager, and the love of my life. You have walked through valleys and climbed mountains with me. I thank God that you are my partner in this life.

Thanks to my daughter. You forever changed me for the better when you made me a mother for the first time. You are beautiful inside and out. You're also a natural-born leader. Please do not doubt yourself and your unique gifts. Always let your heart and light shine for Jesus. Follow your passions and be the change this world needs.

Thanks to my son. We prayed for you for years before you entered the world. You completed our family. I love your smile, your sense of humor, and your gentle and loving spirit. You are a blessing to all who meet you. Be strong and courageous! Always seek God and he will make your path straight.

Thanks to my dear tribe of friends and neighbors in Fort Worth, Texas. I love doing life with you at Christ Chapel Bible Church and Southwest Christian School. I see evidence of the difference you have made in my life and my children's lives every day. I love to travel and visit other places, but I always love to come home.

Thanks to my clients who have allowed me to have a front row seat in their lives. I honestly have learned more from you about living life well, than I have taught you about managing your money. It's a privilege to know you and your families.

Thanks to my literary agent, Esther Fedorkevich, who is now also my friend, for waiting for me, and without whom this book would not be possible.

Finally, thanks to the amazing team of professionals at Zondervan who believed in the message of *Faithful Finance*. I'm especially grateful for my acquisitions editor, Sandra Vander Zicht, and my production editor, Kim Tanner. You took my words on paper and made them better. Your help has been priceless.

Introduction

Come to me, all you who are weary and burdened,
and I will give you rest.

Matthew 11:28

God has laid it on my heart to help guide you on a path to financial freedom. I want to help move you from fearful insecurity to confident control, as it relates to your personal finances. As a financial advisor for two decades, I have observed that financial issues are one of the greatest stressors for both individuals and married couples. Sadly, trouble with money is one of the top three reasons that couples divorce. Issues with money cross all genders, races, and belief systems, proving that the fears associated with money do not discriminate. Those who don't have enough money to provide necessities for their family are often consumed with their personal finances. Surprisingly, those who do have plentiful resources are *also* concerned about their personal finances. You may be surprised to learn that my wealthy clients whom I counsel are often the most fretful people I meet. Those who do not have enough money and those who do have money are both worried about personal financial issues. It's epidemic.

Thank God there is *hope* in Christ. Jesus came so you could have access to *all* of God's blessings and treasures—all of them. My sincere desire is to share with you how to handle your finances so you can live without fear and anxiety.

Money is a tool to be used wisely, and it can be a blessing to you. Those who are obedient to God's plan for their finances will be blessed, and will also be able to bless others. However, God's blessings look different for everyone. Please understand, I'm not preaching a prosperity gospel. I'm not promising that you will be rich beyond your wildest imagination if you believe in Christ, read this book, and follow my advice. However, I do want you to know that you can learn to manage money wisely and live a much more peaceful and fruitful life.

I also want you to know that the God of the Bible is good; the God of the Bible indeed blesses. The God of the Bible is the God who will see us through, regardless of our stressful circumstances. God sometimes blesses our finances, and we raise our hands in thanks. But other times, we experience a lack of resources. Either way, God is always with us. He is watching and waiting for us to trust him, obey him, and learn that in loving him, we have life's deepest blessing.

Are you ready to go on this journey with me? Not only will we study God's Word, but we will also discuss practical ways to manage your finances. We'll discuss how to have discernment when choosing a financial advisor, how to make a monthly budget that actually works for you, how to develop a personal savings plan based on your unique goals, and why learning to give generously will ultimately bless you the most.

I also want to teach you how to reduce your overall debt burden, plan for your children's college years, insure your life so your loved ones are protected, and leave a legacy through estate planning. Most important, however, I want you to discover the *true* source of wealth: a personal relationship with Jesus Christ.

CHAPTER 1

Let a Professional Worry about Your Money So You Don't Have To

> *Plans fail for lack of counsel,*
> *but with many advisers they succeed.*
>
> Proverbs 15:22

I had the privilege of meeting Frank and Diane as clients for the first time in the spring of 2011. They had done an excellent job of managing their personal finances even though they had experienced some very difficult trials in their lives.

Frank worked for a large oil and gas company for thirty-four years, the only client I had who was a lifer at one company. In today's economy, people often move frequently from one position to another at various companies in order to climb the corporate ladder. Not Frank. He went to work for his employer in 1978 and retired on January 1, 2015. As a result, the majority of his net worth was tied up in his 401(k) plan, company pension, and corporate stock. Retirement for Frank was a bit scary because his work was a major part of his identity. That's why he called me three years before he planned to retire. Until that point in his life, his personal financial plan was quite simple: work hard and save as much money as possible. However, he soon realized he needed a professional to coach him through the transition from working full time to retirement. He wanted to have a plan in place, and he certainly did not want to make any hasty decisions.

We held our first meeting at their modest ranch-style home. When I pulled into the driveway, they immediately welcomed me. I soon learned that Frank and Diane had lived in the same home for over twenty years.

After a good bit of time, I asked them, "What are your hopes, dreams, and desires for your retirement years?" Frank was rather young to be a retiree. I envisioned them volunteering at church, traveling, and spending time with family at their lake house. But Frank and Diane's demeanor changed when we started to talk about the future. It seemed to me like they were living the American dream. However, the looks in their eyes left no doubt that something was indeed missing from this Norman Rockwell-like picture.

Diane proceeded to tell me their story. "We have no children," she said. "So there will never be any grandchildren." At age thirteen and age twenty, both of their sons had died suddenly and unexpectedly from previously undetected heart conditions.

By that point in my career, I had counseled many people about how to handle their finances, hearing many personal stories about family dynamics, mismanagement of money, and fear about the future. I honestly thought I had heard it all. However, their story was something I had never heard before, or even imagined. To lose not only one child, but both, was difficult to grasp. How could a good God let this happen to them—twice? Initially, I had no words.

Yet Diane was not bitter. She lived at peace with her circumstances. She didn't pretend that the subject was not painful. However, she certainly was not depressed, angry, bitter, or withdrawn. I asked her that afternoon, "How have you survived the death of each of your sons? I honestly cannot imagine such grief."

She looked at me and said words I will never forget, "Emily, my faith is in Jesus Christ. This is not my home. My earthly life is temporary. I'm at peace knowing that both of my boys loved Jesus. As a parent, that is the most important thing in the world. I know we will be together again, so I have made a conscious choice to never become bitter. I want to make sure my boys recognize me when we meet again in heaven for eternity. If I become angry or bitter, they might not recognize me or know who I am when we are reunited." Diane embodies an amazing testimony of grace, poise, and most important, genuine faith to all who meet her.

As I soon learned, God has continued to use Diane's story to minister to those experiencing great loss and tragedy. This story always makes me think about where I'm headed after this life. Friend, I want us both to spend eternity with our heavenly Father.

Frank also uses their tragedy to bring about good. He teaches a class of young boys at their church, and he often reminds each boy that he is not invincible. He explains that the best gift they can give to their parents is a relationship with Jesus Christ. Through Frank and Diane's lives, God has brought beauty from ashes.

Why People Worry about the Future

Frank and Diane understand the importance of perspective when it comes to making plans for the future, but not everyone has such a solid foundation. In fact, many worry incessantly about the future. That kind of stress robs them of joy today. Fretting about money causes people to lie awake at night, worried about their future. The most common questions I hear regarding money are:

- How will I afford to send my kids to college?

- When will I have enough money saved to be able to retire?
- What will happen if I have an unforeseen illness or disability?
- Do I have enough life insurance to take care of my loved ones if I die before my children are raised?
- Why do I need a will?
- Who can I trust to give me personal financial planning advice?

Can you relate to any of these questions and concerns? Perhaps one, or many, of these questions drove you to read this book. If so, you've already sensed the first secret to faithful finance: *you need to seek wise counsel to help you manage your money well.*

Most of us learn our first money lessons from our parents. If you were blessed to have wise parents who knew how to manage their money well, you likely soaked in some important lessons, such as the need to spend less than you earn, the importance of hard work and planning, and the benefits of having a realistic household budget. However, please remember that learning to manage money well is a lifelong process. Most important, we all need a biblical foundation to understand the importance of putting our knowledge into action. That's why this book highlights not only the financial principles we all need, but also the spiritual foundation that will enable us to put that knowledge to work.

So how can you learn about money? I believe that reading *Faithful Finance* is the perfect first step in your journey. Proverbs 15:22 tells us "many advisers" are necessary for success. I want to encourage you to be a lifelong learner. Scour websites, listen to radio broadcasts, and subscribe to newspapers or magazines that teach you about money. It doesn't have to be an overwhelming process. At the end of this book, I will list some recommended resources that you can utilize to educate yourself further on a variety of topics.

Some people enjoy learning about money and embrace the chance to do so. They like being in the driver's seat and feeling a sense of mastery and control. They truly enjoy receiving advice from wise and successful people around them, from books they read, and from trustworthy websites. At some point, however, most people will benefit from personalized, professional advice tailored to their unique circumstances. That's where seasoned financial advisors like myself can make a huge difference in your long-term financial success.

As a financial advisor, I don't just manage money. I manage relationships with people. I see myself as the quarterback of my client's financial team. My job is to ensure that all of the crucial pieces and advisors are in place for my client's overall financial well-being.

Since I cannot meet with you in person, first see what you can tackle on your own with the help of this book, but please be open to seeking professional help and advice if appropriate for your unique situation. Accountants, investment advisors, insurance brokers, and estate planning attorneys are just some of the professionals you may need as you seek help to manage your personal finances.

My goal for *Faithful Finance* is to give an overview of what a successful financial plan looks like in real, everyday life. I want you, my reader friend, to be empowered. I want you to have the knowledge needed to determine which aspects of your financial plan need immediate attention. It may be that your finances just need a minor tune-up and not a complete overhaul. For example, you may simply need assistance in creating a detailed monthly household budget. As you learn more, and put more pieces of your financial plan into place, you will move from fearful insecurity in dealing with your finances to a feeling of confidence and control.

A Comprehensive Financial Plan

I really wish I could sit down with each and every one of you over a cup of coffee to learn about your life. That is my favorite part of my job. I would love to know your hopes, dreams, goals, and fears as it relates to your personal finances. However, it's just not possible. Since I can't meet with you in person, I will take you through all of the financial planning topics that I typically discuss with my own clients. A comprehensive financial plan will always include the following topics:

- A realistic monthly budget
- A cash reserve plan for unforeseen emergencies
- A plan to tithe and give purposefully and generously
- A debt management strategy
- Specific personal savings goals
- Affordable insurance to protect your loved ones
- Advice about purchasing a home you can afford
- An investment overview
- A strategic retirement plan
- A college savings analysis for children and/or grandchildren if applicable
- A current estate plan

Each of these topics may affect you and your personal finances at some point during your lifetime. Here is a brief overview of what these terms mean and how they relate to you personally.

Monthly Budgets

A monthly budget is a tool used to track monthly income and expenses. It allows an individual or a married couple to take control of their monthly spending habits. The main goal of a monthly budget is to ensure that you have enough money to pay your bills and expenses each month. It also provides a framework to determine how much money is left over each month to begin a savings plan. For more on budgeting, please refer to chapter two.

Cash Reserves

I always recommend that my clients have cash on hand to cover at least three to six months of living expenses. A cash reserve is an emergency fund. It might consist of money in a checking account, savings account, or money market fund. For more details on building a cash reserve account, please refer to chapter two.

Tithing and Giving

The New Testament talks a lot about the importance and benefits of giving. We are to give joyfully as we are able. Why? *Because all of our resources ultimately belong to God.* We're just managers of the assets that he has temporarily given to us. Sometimes that means giving more than ten percent; sometimes that may mean giving less. People often argue about whether the Bible intends for you to give ten percent of your gross income or ten percent of your net income. Honestly, that's between you and God. Tithing is supposed to be a form of worship to God and service to the body of Christ. For more on giving, please refer to chapter three.

Debt Management

This is a crucial part of financial planning. Friend, rest assured that not all debt is bad. This may seem like a foreign concept to some people who subscribe to the philosophy that debt is to be avoided at all cost. I disagree. However, you must be very prudent when using debt to improve your overall net worth. Examples of debt that can actually help improve your long-term financial future, and overall net worth, are the following:

- Student loans, which can allow a person to get an education so they can dramatically increase their earning potential over their lifetime. A person's ability to work and generate an income is their greatest asset.

- Small business loans to start a viable business.
- A mortgage loan to purchase a home, which is an appreciating asset. A home may be one of the largest investments an individual or a couple will make in their lifetime. If you never purchase a home, you will always be enslaved to a landlord as a renter.

Please, please understand that I'm not a proponent of taking on debt that you cannot afford. However, there are certain circumstances when debt is not all bad news. For more information on debt management, please refer to chapter four.

Personal Savings Goals

Goals are extremely important because they give you direction. If you do not have a plan, you will inevitably lose focus. As a result, you won't make wise decisions with your finances. There is a major difference between savings needs and savings wants. For example, you may *need* to save for your retirement and your children's college tuition. You also may *want* to save for a new car or a lake house. Both types of goals are good. However, savings *needs* should always take precedence over savings *wants*. For more on saving, please refer to chapter five.

Insurance Needs

The purpose of insurance is to protect yourself and your family's finances. You can purchase insurance for life, health, long-term care, or disability from a licensed insurance agent and/or a financial advisor. You're probably most familiar with insurance for your personal property such as a home, car, or boat. In most circumstances, insurance is not an investment; it is an expense. One exception to this rule is certain types of life insurance. However, for the most part, you want to provide insurance for yourself and your family for as little cost as possible. For more information on life insurance, disability insurance, and long-term care insurance, please refer to chapter six.

Purchasing a Home

As I mentioned previously, a home may be one of the largest investments an individual or a couple will make in their lifetime. Believe it or not, it is possible to consider the practical housing needs of your family *and* make a very wise investment. As with all investments, ideally you want your asset to grow and increase in value without a great deal of volatility. In the financial world, we call this "upside growth potential with downside protection." For many, a home will represent a large percentage of their assets and overall net worth. For more information on prudent strategies for buying a home, please refer to chapter seven.

Investments

This is a very broad topic, with more options for investing money today than ever before. Investing can be overwhelming if you're not working with a professional money manager. However, please do not be discouraged if you're just starting to save money. I will outline simple ways to begin investing—like purchasing well-diversified mutual funds. For more information, please refer to chapter eight.

Retirement Planning

Ideally, an individual or a couple will begin planning and saving for retirement early in their careers. The earlier you begin saving for retirement, the less you will have to save each month, because you will be able to take advantage of the beauty of compound interest. We'll discuss retirement planning and how to transition into retirement in much greater detail in chapter eight.

Saving for College

Once you become a parent, you're responsible for the health, maintenance, and welfare of your child. Many parents also feel responsible for providing higher education for their child. While not every child will benefit from a four-year college degree, many will need some sort of additional training beyond high school, whether that is at a community college, a trade school, or the military. If you're planning to help your child or grandchild with continuing education expenses, the sooner you get started on saving and investing, the better. For more information on financial products available to help save for college, please refer to chapter nine.

Estate Planning

Estate planning consists of wills, trusts, medical directives, and the organization of your financial affairs. You may need to work with a licensed estate-planning attorney to ensure that your wishes and desires are carried out upon your death. Yes, it sounds morbid. However, I encourage my clients to embrace the fact that one of the best gifts they can give to their family is to have their financial affairs in order. Estate planning is covered in chapter ten.

A Personalized Financial Plan: Frank and Diane

There are a lot of topics to cover to make sure your personal finances are properly managed. Obviously, someone who is single, in their twenties, and renting has less complicated finances than someone in their forties, who is married with children and simultaneously trying to pay off a house, save for retirement, and put away money for college. But whatever your life stage and needs, a professional financial advisor can help you plan for the best life possible by pointing out what you are doing right, where you need help, and what you might want to do next.

By now, I imagine you're probably wondering what proper financial planning looks like in real, everyday life. You're probably also wondering if having a financial advisor would be helpful in your own situation. After all, everyone's situation is different.

In order to illustrate how a financial advisor could help you, let me outline the various ways we organized Frank and Diane's financial lives to get them ready for retirement. They both continue to heal as they embrace a retirement that doesn't look like what they envisioned in their younger years. However, there has been redemption in their lives, and God has blessed them as they have continued to be faithful, even during very difficult trials.

Budget

Frank and Diane created a detailed budget for all of their expected monthly expenses during retirement. I then reviewed their budget to make sure they had not overlooked any key items such as travel, insurance premiums due twice per year, or annual property taxes. To make sure it was realistic, they practiced living on this new budget for a year before Frank actually retired.

Tithing and Giving

A tithe was already part of Frank and Diane's monthly budget and spiritual beliefs, but they also wanted advice on the many options for giving beyond their tithe, both in their lifetime and after they passed away. We discussed how to create a legacy and the best way to honor their sons with their financial resources by helping others.

Mortgage Debt

When Frank first retired, we used a lump sum of cash from his 401(k) plan to pay off their mortgage so they could live debt free. Their only housing expenses would be monthly utilities, homeowner's insurance, and property taxes. They plan to stay in their existing home as long as possible, and in our planning, we took that desire into account.

Insurance

Like many couples, Frank and Diane were concerned about their future health care needs if either one of them ever needed to enter an assisted living facility or nursing home. To address that concern, I helped Frank and Diane apply for long-term care insurance to take care of any medical needs not covered by Medicare or traditional health insurance. They didn't need disability insurance since they were entering their retirement years.

They also had enough cash and securities in savings and retirement plans, that they no longer needed life insurance to cover shortfalls. In other words, they were "self-insured." As for medical insurance, they eventually planned to use Medicare once they reached age sixty-five. In the meantime, Frank was fortunate to be able to maintain corporate medical insurance during retirement.

Investments and Retirement Income

Frank, Diane, and I put an investment plan in place that is well diversified. We wanted their assets to keep up with inflation and have upside potential. However, we also needed to provide their investment portfolio with downside protection since they are now retired. In this particular situation, we annuitized a portion of Frank and Diane's assets in order to create a guaranteed income stream that they will never outlive. In our planning, we also considered the tax ramifications of their investments. Finally, we looked at what money would be coming in from Social Security and decided at what age each of them should claim their benefits.

Will

At my suggestion, Frank and Diane met with an estate-planning attorney to update their wills and trusts. They are both charitably minded and wanted to ensure their estate would provide resources for some close relatives when they both passed away. In addition, I asked them what their passions were. They both mentioned a desire to create scholarships for college students attending their late son's alma mater. In addition, they wanted to support their church financially, even after they were no longer living. By creating a detailed estate plan with their attorney, they were assured that their legacy would live on long after they passed away.

Life Advice

I like to encourage people to plan for living, not dying. I urged Frank and Diane to enjoy the fruits of their hard work. Knowing they enjoyed traveling, I told them, "Go see the world. Check off some items on your bucket list." I'm happy to report that they did go on a two-week Alaskan vacation during the first year of Frank's retirement. They have now also visited Hawaii and spent many weekends at their lake house. It thrills me to know they are truly enjoying their retirement years.

Finding a Financial Advisor

I hope Frank and Diane's story encourages you to seek wise counsel from a trusted financial advisor, someone who can help you with the complex issues involved in creating a comprehensive financial plan. Pray about the person whom you will hire to help navigate your path to financial security. Ask people you trust for personal recommendations. As James reminds us, "If any of you lacks wisdom, you should ask God, who gives generously to all without finding fault, and it will be given to you" (James 1:5).

Professional Designations

One question I'm often asked is this: What qualities should I look for when interviewing prospective financial advisors? It may seem very difficult to choose an advisor among the thousands of people working in this industry. Advisors understand this dilemma, so they have tried to differentiate themselves with various professional designations. These designations are displayed as three letters after the advisor's name, indicating which advisors have gone that extra step to make themselves qualified professionals.

Most designations are earned through required coursework and examinations that test an advisor's knowledge in various specialized areas. Some designations are specifically designed for financial advisors who work with retirees, while other designations show specialization in insurance or business. No two designations are exactly the same. Some designations are definitely more renowned than others. If you don't know what a designation stands for and what it means, it can be difficult to know if the person is qualified to manage your money and give you sound financial planning advice. The Financial Industry Regulatory Authority (FINRA) has an online resource that defines the various professional designations that advisors may hold. You can find this information at http://www.finra.org/investors/professional-designations. The following is a list of well-respected credentials that financial advisors may hold and what the initials stand for:

1. Certified Public Accountant (CPA): This is by far the oldest and most established financial credential. The CPA designation has long been widely recognized as the definitive credential for tax expertise.

2. Certified Financial Planner (CFP): This is the most widely recognized credential in the financial planning industry.

3. Chartered Life Underwriter (CLU) and Chartered Financial Consultant (ChFC): Both of these designations were originally created by the life insurance industry.

4. Chartered Financial Analyst (CFA): This designation is generally considered to be one of the most difficult and prestigious credentials in the financial industry, at least in terms of investment management.

In my case, the letters after my name are MBA and CFA. MBA stands for Master of Business Administration. I earned this degree from Texas Christian University (TCU) in 1998. Only individuals who have finished the coursework required for a business graduate degree through an accredited university can use the three letters MBA after their name. In addition, you typically cannot enter a masters program to earn an MBA if you have not first earned a four-year bachelor's degree.

The second set of initials after my name is CFA, which stands for Chartered Financial Analyst. I earned my CFA charter in 2002. The CFA designation is only awarded after the completion of three independent exams, usually occurring annually. The process is rigorous and demanding. In fact, during the period of 1963 through 2016, approximately 1.4 million people have taken the first level of the CFA exam and only forty-two percent have passed. Additionally, over the same period, the pass rates for levels two and three are forty-six percent and fifty-eight percent, respectively. The rigor of the exams ensures that the only candidates who pass are the candidates that should pass. Thus, of the approximately 1.4 million candidates who have taken at least Level 1 of the CFA exam, only 209,000 candidates have actually passed all three levels and earned their CFA Charter. Finally, and what is even more amazing, the percentage of women compared to men who earned a CFA globally is only nineteen percent.[1] Just like any other financial advisor who has worked hard to differentiate themselves, I hope that understanding the value of the CFA designation will help investors, readers, and my clients to recognize the significance of the knowledge that I can bring to help them manage their personal finances.

Doing Due Diligence

I want to encourage you to review the educational background and years of experience of the advisor you choose to manage your money. They should be well credentialed, not merely a good sales person. Check to make sure the advisor's security licenses are in good standing and that they have no fines or complaints filed against them. Some people in the financial services industry have taken intensive sales training programs. They can sell ice to an Alaskan. However, they don't have the knowledge, education, and experience required to truly provide you with wise counsel. As we say in Texas, "They are all hat and no cattle."

Please remember, if something sounds too good to be true, it probably is! A prospective financial advisor should not ever recommend a get-rich-quick scheme. Instead, they should recommend that you save money systematically over time in a disciplined manner. In addition, your money should be invested in a well-diversified portfolio. Please educate yourself and do your own research before you agree to any investment portfolio recommendations for your hard-earned money.

I would also encourage you to ask financially trustworthy, successful people for a referral. It's always best to interview a financial advisor who has already worked for people whom you know and trust. For high-net-worth individuals and people approaching retirement, I recommend using a fee-based financial advisor. Fee-based financial advisors do well financially if you do well, because they are paid a percentage of the value of the dollars that they actually invest. In the financial world, we call these dollars *assets under management*. The advisor's compensation will increase *only* if your assets increase in value. If your account loses value, the fee-based financial advisor also earns *less* money. This prevents any conflicts of interest. The annual fee charged by an advisor is usually around one percent of the assets under management.

If you're just starting out, or your finances are not that complicated, you may want to pay an hourly fee for one or two meetings to discuss a couple of specific holes in your financial situation. This would be the same concept as using an attorney that charges by the hour. You only pay them for the actual hours you meet with them.

I want to caution you about hiring a commission-based money manager, commonly known as a stockbroker. They only make money when they buy or sell a position in your portfolio. It may or may not be in your best interest for them to be constantly trading positions in your accounts. We call this "churning and burning." It's not a good thing.

Another tip I have for you is to confirm that your new financial advisor has relationships with accountants and estate planning attorneys. It's always a best practice for all three advisors to coordinate your financial plan. You really need to know both the legal and tax ramifications of your investments.

It's optimal if your financial advisor is licensed to sell investments as well as insurance products. Life insurance, disability insurance, and long-term care insurance are very important aspects of your comprehensive financial plan. I also suggest that you work with a professional financial advisor that isn't captive to one company. It's in your best interest for your advisor to shop among a variety of financial service institutions, ensuring that you receive the highest quality products for your hard-earned money.

Finally, your financial advisor should be a person you truly like and want to spend time with. Your advisor should have an attitude of collaboration with you—not pressing their advice on you, but being open to understanding where you're coming from and what values are most important to you and your family. If you don't understand something, they should be willing to take the time and spend the effort to teach you. They should never pressure you to buy a product or investment you don't fully understand or feel comfortable with. Trust your instincts when you meet with potential financial advisors. If the relationship is successful, they will become a major part of your life, one of the first people you call when any major life transitions occur, such as a change in job, the birth of a child, or the approach of retirement.

Finally, my reader friend, I truly want to encourage you to be proactive and seek wise counsel with your personal finances. Educating yourself about finances and finding a trusted advisor is the first secret to moving you from fearful insecurity to confident control as it relates to your finances.

CHAPTER 2

Cash Is King (or Queen)

SECRET #2: THE FAITHFUL CREATE A BUDGET AND BUILD UP A CASH RESERVE

*The plans of the diligent lead to profit
as surely as haste leads to poverty.*

Proverbs 21:5

I first learned the importance of budgeting and having a cash reserve during graduate school. Trust me, I have never forgotten that important lesson.

After I graduated with a bachelor's degree from Texas A&M University, I enrolled in a full-time MBA program at Texas Christian University (TCU) in Fort Worth. As a result, I am an Aggie *and* a Horned Frog. In Texas, we call this dual citizenship.

My parents were very generous to provide for my living expenses and my tuition as an undergraduate student. Upon graduation, my parents proudly shook my hand, congratulated me on all of my hard work, and joyfully told me I was on my own financially. My father literally skipped down the street. He kept shouting, "I just got a raise. Hallelujah! Both of my children are out of college." He called it Independence Day.

Sigh.

Needless to say, I was not nearly as excited as he was.

After graduation, I immediately started waitressing to earn

35

money while I waited to find out if I had been accepted to graduate school. I really thought I had things under control financially when they awarded me a scholarship to pay for my tuition for two years while I attended the master's program. However, I didn't know at the time that my fees and books were not covered by my scholarship. Unfortunately, I wasn't prepared for those unexpected expenses. At the time, there were two separate checkout lines at the TCU bookstore for students to pay for their books. The first line was for students with Frog Bucks that enabled them to charge their books to their parents' account. Students were very happy-go-lucky in that line. But there was also a second line for students who were paying for their own books. I stood in that second line—the place where the real world got very real for me.

In order to keep my scholarship at TCU, I had to work on campus at least ten hours per week. I hardly had any margin in my week after I went to class, worked on campus, met with my peers for group projects, studied for exams, and read the required reading material. The first few months of graduate school, I managed to squeak by on the money I'd made during the previous summer waiting tables. But by Christmastime I was almost broke.

I eventually finished my final exams after the first brutal semester of graduate school. All of us newbies in the MBA program were completely exhausted, sleep deprived, and barely able to think straight when our final exams were over. Then our professors handed us what they called a "Christmas bonus." Unfortunately, it was not the financial kind. Our professors informed us that we had a group project to complete in three days. It was a Harvard Business Review case study where we had to read, analyze, and then present our findings to the faculty. They divided us into teams of five. I was the only member of my team who was not married or did not have a roommate. Everyone agreed that my apartment would be the best place to set up shop since we would be awake for the majority of the next seventy-two hours. We took turns napping.

And so it began.

My electricity was on almost twenty-four hours per day for three days. All of the lights in my apartment were on, multiple computers were plugged in, and my team members turned on my air conditioner during the day when they got hot. Then they would get cold at night and turn on the heater. Back and forth— hot to cold—for three days. Why not? They weren't paying for the electricity in my apartment.

I got my monthly electric bill a few days after I went home to my parents' house for the Christmas holidays. Unfortunately, I didn't have enough money in my checking account to pay the bill. I was now officially flat broke. So I immediately had to get a job over the Christmas holidays to make enough money to keep the electricity on in my apartment. My dreams of relaxing and recuperating from the difficult first semester of graduate school quickly shattered. Before the second semester began, I knew I would have to get another job in order to survive financially. Eventually, I figured out how to make it all work, but it wasn't easy by any means. Desperation became a great motivator.

I landed a second job working for American Express Financial Advisors (now Ameriprise Financial) as an intern. Ironically, that's where my financial planning career began. If I had not been completely broke, I never would have agreed to take on another job, in addition to my on-campus job, and my full-time graduate school schedule.

God had a plan all along.

Creating a Budget

A lot of the stress I experienced in graduate school resulted from the fact that I owed more in monthly bills than I had in cash, savings, or from my monthly earnings. Friend, I don't want you to end up in the same situation that I was in while attending graduate school. Trust me, it's such a stressful way to live your life. I don't want you, my reader friend, to be living one flat tire, medical bill, or broken household appliance away from financial devastation.

Now take a deep breath. I have good news for you. There is *hope* and there are ways to be proactive with your finances, rather than reactive. Proper financial planning is the key to avoiding many financial pitfalls. The most basic financial planning task, but the most critical for success, is creating a realistic monthly budget.

I want to encourage you to see creating a budget as a way to be responsible and respectful of the resources that God has entrusted to you. What you give attention to in your life is what you will gain affection for. What you have affection for changes your activities and attitude. If you truly love God and want to show affection for him, one of the ways to do that is to actively and responsibly manage your personal finances.

If you have a realistic monthly budget that you commit to and actually follow, it will allow you to live a more fruitful and peaceful life from a financial standpoint. You will have a much better handle on how much income is coming in to your household and how much money is being spent each month. Also, careful budgeting ultimately allows you to give a portion of your income to kingdom causes, such as your local church or nonprofit organizations, because you're not spending more money than you earn. There are missionaries, pastors, and nonprofit organizations all over the world that are currently acting as the hands and feet of Christ by serving God's people. They could truly benefit from your financial support so they can continue to do the kingdom work God has called them to do. Stop and pray right now about whether or not your budget is being properly managed. Do you currently have a tithe or financial offering as part of your monthly budget? If not, consider starting with a small portion of your income each month and see if God blesses your finances. We'll talk more about tithing and giving in chapter three.

From a practical standpoint, a budget is simply a written plan, or spreadsheet, that shows you in detail how much money you earn from all sources each month, how much you need to live on, and how much discretionary income you can allocate toward your savings goals, tithing, and treating yourself.

No matter what your age or stage in life, you will never out-grow the need for a budget. *The most important thing you can do to move from fearful insecurity regarding your personal finances to confi-dent control, is to create and live by a monthly budget.*

Friend, do you know how much money you spend each month? If not, please don't be embarrassed. That accomplishes nothing. Let's figure it out together. I suggest going to an all-cash system for a couple of months to track your expenses. If you're very disciplined, you can use something as simple as a shoebox to store and save every single receipt for a month. Do not exclude any receipts or expenses. I suggest you place the shoebox next to the door of your home. Then empty your receipts from your purse or wallet every time you come home. If you spend $4.50 at your local coffee shop, then save the receipt. This is the only way to truly know how much money you're spending each month. After this, you'll be able to determine how much discretionary income you have. Discretionary income is the amount of money you can afford to save or spend each month after all of your expenses are paid. Be prepared to be surprised. Many people are shocked to find out how much money they spend on miscellaneous items like lattes, dining out, shopping, or entertainment. None of these expenses are bad. You just need to make sure you're spending *less* than you make. People often go over their monthly budget one small purchase at a time. Small purchases can really add up over time when you're swiping credit cards and/or not paying attention to what you're spending throughout the month.

Friend, one of the most fundamental financial planning goals is to have money left over at the end of each month. Then you can allocate it toward your savings goals and even toward some purchases or activities you enjoy, such as new shoes or dinner with friends.

Suggested Budget Percentages According to Budget Categories

In order for a budget to actually work and benefit your family, it has to be tailored to your unique lifestyle and situation. I have included two resources that give realistic suggestions on how to begin your budgeting process by category.

The first suggestion source is *The Total Money Makeover* by Dave Ramsey. The second suggested source is *Money Matters* by Larry Burkett.

Suggested Budget Percentages According to Budget Categories

	TOTAL MONEY MAKEOVER SUGGESTIONS	MONEY MATTERS SUGGESTIONS
Charitable Gifts	10-15%	10%
Savings	5-10%	10%
Housing	25-35%	32%
Utilities	5-10%	(Included in housing)
Food	5-15%	13%
Transportation	10-15%	13%
Clothing	2-7%	5%
Medical/Health	5-10%	4%
Personal	5-10%	13%
Recreation	5-10%	6%
Debt	5-10%	5%

Building Up a Cash Reserve

As a professional financial advisor, I help others de-stress regarding their finances so they never find themselves in the situation I did that first year of graduate school. The very first question I ask my clients when we sit down for our initial conversation is, "How much cash do you have on hand?" It really doesn't matter if they want to talk about retirement planning or whether or not they have enough life insurance if they have no liquid assets. *One of the greatest stressors in personal finances is living overextended.* This is one of the reasons that credit cards were invented, but they can quickly become a quagmire if you rely too much on credit to bail you out of every emergency. People who live paycheck to paycheck, or who keep putting unforeseen expenses on their credit card, will never get ahead financially. Only those who have a cash reserve account will have the money they need when there are unforeseen expenses. I can promise you this: You are not in control. Things will break; people will get sick; and disasters will happen. If your health suddenly deteriorates or you receive a very large unexpected electric bill like I did, life will be very stressful without any cash to fall back on to pay for those expenses.

Rest assured, it's not all bad news. You absolutely *can* plan for these unforeseen types of events in advance. If you have at least three months' worth of living expenses in cash, then life will become much less stressful. There is a lot of truth in the old saying, "Everything in life is easier with a little cash." Let's talk about the best way to build up an adequate cash reserve, and what to do with your cash once you have it in the bank.

Step 1

Review your monthly budget to determine exactly how much you're spending each month. I have created a detailed monthly budget worksheet for your reference at the end of this chapter.

You may also choose to create and monitor your monthly budget online using tools like Mint, Quicken, or EveryDollar. Before you invest in an online budgeting program, be sure that your bank supports it and will import financial transactions into that program. Some banks will do this transaction for free, while others will charge a small fee.

Step 2

After carefully reviewing your budget, identify which expenses you regularly incur that are unnecessary. For example, eating out at restaurants and going to the movies are not necessary for your daily survival. These are called discretionary expenses. Once your discretionary expenses have been identified, try to forgo as many of those expenses as possible. Use the money you would have spent on discretionary expenses to start funding a cash reserve account.

Remember friend, these activities are not bad; you just don't need these activities in order to survive. Try to think of ways to entertain yourself without spending money. Go for a walk; visit public parks; enjoy local playgrounds if you have children or grandchildren; attend activities at your local church; read a library book; or call a friend. You can even check out movies at the library for free. Get creative.

Step 3

Take an inventory of your possessions. Do you own anything you no longer need, use, or want that could be valuable to someone else? You may be able to clean out some clutter in your home and turn it into cash by holding a garage sale or selling your name-brand clothes at a consignment store. With the popularity of buy/sell sites such as Facebook, eBay, and Craigslist, it's easier than ever before to sell your gently used or never-used items and turn them into cash.

Step 4

Look for ways to boost your income. Take on a part-time job, offer your talents and services to friends or neighbors for a fee, or sign up for overtime hours. Working harder now offers the benefit of finding peace later; so remind yourself that you're working not just for money, but also to build confident control.

I have several friends that have helped add to their household incomes and cash reserve accounts by using their gifts and talents to earn extra money. My dear friend Julia is a very talented seamstress. She has become the "go-to" person in our town for all things you could ever want or imagine being monogrammed. This has always been a hobby of hers, and now she makes money doing something she loves. Some other dear friends of mind, Annette and her daughter Grace, make the most delicious cinnamon rolls I've ever eaten. They now take orders at Christmastime for cinnamon rolls. They too have turned a hobby into a nice little business.

Step 5

Open a savings account at your local bank that is separate from your regular checking account, so the funds don't comingle. Why? Because it's so tempting to spend extra cash that sits in your regular checking account. This new savings account is now earmarked for emergencies only, or what is often called a "rainy day fund." This is *not* "fun money" for splurging on a vacation, nor is it a savings fund for a new car. It is for emergencies *only*.

Step 6

Continue to save your discretionary income until you have at least three months' worth of living expenses in your new savings account.

Step 7

Relax and enjoy your new financial freedom in regards to unforeseen expenses.

Additional Advice

Soon enough, an emergency financial need will pop up that requires you to spend money from your cash reserve account. It is then important to go back through the above steps to once again build up your cash reserve fund. Once again, be purposeful and mindful about reducing and/or eliminating your discretionary purchases. Consider working more and direct all savings into your cash reserve fund until it's fully replenished. Your cash reserve account is your first line of defense. Friend, please don't drain this account or you will leave yourself vulnerable to serious financial difficulties.

If you're self-employed or worried about your job stability, consider setting aside six months' worth of living expenses instead of just three. This is also a good benchmark for those who work on commission only. If your income fluctuates from month to month, you'll be better prepared to handle any swings in your income if you have adequate cash on hand.

After you have three months of cash in your savings account, don't stop saving! You have now become much more disciplined in managing your monthly budget. Most likely, you haven't even missed the funds you've been saving each month. Now is the time to consider contributing your regular monthly savings to a new savings goal, whether that's a house, retirement, or your child's college fund. Saving money for future goals is critical to gaining financial security and confident control. We'll discuss saving and investing in much more detail in chapter five and chapter eight.

My prayer for you is that you will be encouraged and inspired to create a workable budget, and to build up and maintain a cash reserve account. I want you to be protected from financial hardships in the future by being proactive with your finances now. Please take some time to complete the detailed budget worksheet at the end of this chapter. It's the first step you can take today to gain control of your money.

If you would rather have an electronic copy of this budget worksheet, simply log on to my website www.emilygstroud.com and enter your email address when prompted. I will be more than happy to send you a complimentary electronic version you can use to fill in the blanks on your own computer.

Last but not least, always remember the following: "The plans of the diligent lead to profit as surely as haste [and negligence!] leads to poverty" (Prov. 21:5, notation mine).

Monthly Budget Worksheet
Monthly Cost

Housing

Mortgage or Rent	
Second Mortgage or Rent	
Phone	
Electricity	
Gas	
Water & Sewer	
Cable	
Waste Removal	
Maintenance & Repairs	
Supplies or Decorations	
Other Housing Expenses	
Subtotals	

Food

Groceries	
Dining Out	
Other	
Subtotals	

Transportation

Vehicle 1 Payment	
Vehicle 2 Payment	
Bus/Taxi Fare	
Auto Insurance	
Auto Licensing	
Fuel	
Car Maintenance & Repairs	
Other	
Subtotals	

Gifts & Donations

Tithe to Church	
Gift to Charity	
Other Gifts	
Subtotals	

EMILY G. STROUD
TRUE WEALTH COMES FROM GOD

Children

Medical

Clothing

School Tuition

School Supplies

Sports or
Organization
Dues/Fees

Lunch Money

Child Care

Toys/Games

Other

Subtotals

Pets

Veterinarian Bills

Food

Toys

Medical

Grooming

Subtotals

Entertainment

Video/DVD

CDs

Movies

Concerts

Sporting Events

Live Theater

Other

Subtotals

Loans

Personal

Student

Credit Card

Credit Card

Credit Card

Other

Subtotals

EMILY G. STROUD
TRUE WEALTH COMES FROM GOD

Savings or Investments

Retirement Account	
Investment Account	
College	
Other	
Subtotals	

Legal

Attorney	
Alimony	
Payments on Lien or Judgment	
Other	
Subtotals	

Taxes

Federal	
State	
Local	
Other	
Subtotals	

Miscellaneous

Travel Expenses	
Haircuts/ Manicures/ Grooming	
Other Expenses Not Mentioned Above	
Subtotals	

Insurance

Home	
Health	
Life	
Other	
Subtotals	

Monthly Income

Income 1	
Income 2	
Extra Income (trust, royalties, etc.)	
Total Monthly Income	

Discretionary Income Calculation

Total Monthly Income - All Sources	
Total Monthly Expenses - All Categories	
Discretionary Income	

EMILY G. STROUD
TRUE WEALTH COMES FROM GOD

CHAPTER 3

God Is a Good Gift Giver

SECRET #3: THE FAITHFUL GIVE GENEROUSLY AND PRAYERFULLY

Every good and perfect gift is from above, coming down from the Father of the heavenly lights, who does not change like shifting shadows.

James 1:17

My friends Mike and Jessica are all about God's economy. They take their calling to provide for others extremely seriously. We recently met to discuss their thoughts and beliefs on giving generously. They were kind enough to share their thoughts openly and honestly with me. They have learned through life circumstances that giving generously and prayerfully is a key to moving from fearful insecurity to confident control, when it relates to personal finances.

Jessica is the daughter of a pastor who has always had a huge heart for others, but limited financial means. Jessica's parents modeled generosity by giving freely with their time and their resources. Jessica also had the opportunity to go into the mission field right out of high school. She was born with the spirit of generosity, but she had no idea how that would play out.

While working as a missionary in orphanages in Asia, she learned the gift of compassion. She spent time rocking malnourished toddlers who had been tied to chairs with string. No one touched them, so they failed to thrive. Jessica went from chair to chair untying these babies, feeding them, rocking them, and praying over them. The worst part? She had to tie the toddlers up again before she left.

From that point on, she knew she could not pretend that suffering was not happening in the world—locally, nationally, and internationally. Jessica has always believed that giving is not just something you do with a portion of your income and time. Instead, she believed that giving was her God-given purpose and the reason for living.

In 1998, she met her soon-to-be husband Mike. However, his background and spiritual gifts were far different from Jessica's. Mike was born into a family of entrepreneurs. His parents taught him how to run a business successfully, but they never taught him much about generosity. Mike's grandparents had lived through the Great Depression. As a result, the legacy in Mike's family passed down for generations was to save as much as possible in case another financial catastrophe ever happened again. Mike's family taught him to live in protection mode.

Mike and Jessica have been married for over seventeen years now. They have experienced huge financial success, as the world would see it. However, their business ventures have not always thrived, and they have not always lived on easy street.

After they got married, Mike and Jessica bought a small business in a rural town in Texas and lived in a studio apartment. They struggled financially for many years. Mike spent a lot of time, energy, and sweat equity getting his business off the ground and making it profitable. A few years later, it finally generated enough income for Mike to net a modest profit. They were not wealthy by any means, but they were finally living a comfortable, middle-class lifestyle.

During that time, they made the decision to give above and

beyond their tithe. They began to give sacrificially, regardless of how Mike's business performed. Along the way, some crippling blows to the US economy devastated their financial reserves. Had they not given so generously, they may have had enough money to keep their business afloat. Mike grew angry with God. He questioned why God would allow this devastation when he and Jessica had been so faithful to give sacrificially. The irony of God's plan and provision came later, after they had sold the failing company and invested in a new one.

As God would have it, by obediently tithing and giving as the Holy Spirit prompted, Mike and Jessica received the biggest financial blessing of their lifetime. A year after they sold the doomed business, their new business venture catapulted their income beyond their wildest dreams. They became millionaires in less than a year. Mike and Jessica then read *The Hole in Our Gospel* by the president of World Vision, Richard Stearns. They had been very faithful to give a tithe and an offering throughout their marriage. But this book inspired and encouraged them to give even more sacrificially.

Stearns teaches in this book that God's answer to poverty is us. So Mike and Jessica began to give sacrificially, way above and beyond their ten percent tithe. The Lord used the book to open their eyes to the fact that they had been given abundant resources—not to hoard for their family, but to give to those in need. As they accumulated more wealth, they became increasingly aware that there was no sports car, mansion, airplane, or vacation home that came close to the eternal joy of giving to others in Christ's name.

It turned out that God was indeed blessing Mike and Jessica for their sacrificial giving. God actually *saved* Mike and Jessica from financial ruin *through* their generosity. Had they not been giving sacrificially, they would have had enough cash on hand to keep the original business that is now closed and worth nothing.

The blessings of their faithful, sacrificial giving have been monumental both financially and spiritually.

Please understand that I'm not encouraging you to give away so much money that you go bankrupt. I'm also not encouraging you to be irresponsible with your finances. However, I am encouraging you to give sacrificially and prayerfully. Mike and Jessica have inspired me by their faithfulness with their personal finances. They are investing in kingdom causes and not stuff.

God, the Giver of Good Gifts

The best news I have for you is that our God is a good gift giver. Many people believe they cannot afford to tithe to their church or give to those in need. They're fearful that they won't be able to meet their own needs if they give money to others. I have witnessed in both my life and the lives of many others, that God ultimately provides for all of our needs. It may just look different than how we imagined.

Part of achieving financial freedom is understanding that you will never prosper if you do not love others as God has loved you. I love what Mother Teresa had to say about giving: "It is not about how much we give, but about how much love we put into giving." You do not have to look very far to find people who are in need. Unfortunately, our natural, sinful nature is to look away, or run away, if we encounter people in need. Helping others can be messy, and we often don't want to be inconvenienced. However, Christ commanded us to show compassion and meet the needs as we see them, without expecting anything in return. "If anyone has material possessions and sees a brother or sister in need but has no pity on them, how can the love of God be in that person?" (1 John 3:17).

If we greet others with open hands, we will be opening our hands to accept new gifts from God as well. Author and motivational speaker Zig Ziglar developed a personal credo throughout his life and career that closely resembles Philippians 2:4, "You can have everything in life you want if you will just help enough other people get what they want." To help yourself, you must first help others.

Ultimately, all of your resources belong to God. You are just a steward of the assets he has entrusted you with. If you cannot be trusted to manage a small amount of money wisely, then why would God trust you with much? Jesus said, "Whoever can be trusted with very little can also be trusted with much, and whoever is dishonest with very little will also be dishonest with much" (Luke 16:10).

Time and Tithe

There is a lot written regarding the rules of tithing and the amount you are supposed to tithe. Historically, there have been many discussions about whether the Bible intends for you to give ten percent of your gross income (includes *all* income from all revenue sources) or ten percent of your net income (revenue minus expenses and taxes).

I've also read articles discussing whether it's considered "stealing from God" to split your ten percent tithe between the church and other charities. Another common debate is whether or not your acts of service count as a tithe. Honestly, I believe that how you spend both your money and your time is between you and God. Tithing is supposed to be a form of worship to God and a service to the body of Christ. If you focus too much on the rules of giving, you may become more focused on legalism rather than faith. At times, God may encourage you to give to a special situation, or an urgent need of someone in the body of Christ. As a result, you may give more than ten percent of your income. This is called an offering. It's money that you give over and above your ten percent tithe to the church. Then there may be extenuating circumstances during certain seasons of your life, which may mean giving less or not at all. Instead, you'll be the recipient of gifts and offerings from others as you handle an unforeseen crisis in your own life.

A friend of mine went through a medical crisis a few years ago that put a large financial strain on her family. Her husband had been laid off from his job for several months, and then she was unexpectedly diagnosed with breast cancer. Although they had always tithed faithfully, during this crisis there was no way for them to tithe. Instead, they relied on God and his people to provide for their needs, and their faith was encouraged as they saw many people give sacrificially, to help them in their time of need.

You may be surprised to hear this, but God does not need your money. He is God. However, what he wants is a relationship with you and your heart. He wants you to be content with what you have and to give without compulsion. God wants you to be committed to giving generously, even if it's not popular, easy, or financially profitable for you. Typically, people who give generously to their church and to those in need, grow both spiritually and emotionally in the following ways:

- Faith grows as you trust God with your resources.
- Depression and anxiety decrease as you learn to trust God more and worry less about the future.
- You are blessed by being a part of something bigger than yourself. This results in a sense of community with others.
- Giving guards against the sin of selfishness.

As you learn to give generously, you will also become more content, regardless of the circumstances around you. This contentment is only found in Christ. Contentment does not mean complacency. True contentment occurs when you're not using material goods, exotic vacations, or entertainment to try to fill a void in your heart.

According to Pastor Rick Warren:

> It feels good to give generously—it really does. A person who doesn't understand that has never given generously. The happiest people in the world are the most giving people. Guilt never motivates people to give. Giving that is motivated by guilt only lasts as long as the guilt does. So you never use guilt to motivate people to give. You use joy to motivate people to give.
>
> I absolutely do not accept the health and wealth theology, which teaches that God wants everybody to be rich. But the fact is, there are more promises in the Bible related to giving than any other subject. You cannot out-give God. If you're going to be Christlike you've got to learn to give…. Giving by revelation means I determine my gift by praying, "Lord, what do you want to give through me?" This requires faith. When you give by revelation, you're committing an act of worship and saying, "How much am I willing to trust God?"[1]

A Plan for Giving

Let's talk about how to set up a plan for giving systematically, so it's a regular part of your budget to tithe and give to those in need. I do believe it will become a true joy in your life if you're faithful to give to God's church and his people regularly.

Step 1

Choose to tithe *not* out of fear, guilt, or legalism, but because you love God. As believers in Christ, we're called to honor and trust him, even if he doesn't do anything for us in return. He does not owe us anything. The focus of tithing isn't money, but rather the condition of our hearts.

Step 2

Be brave when you receive your next paycheck. Take ten percent off the top and ask God to bless your tithe to the benefit of his kingdom. To take it one step further, consider automating your charitable giving and tithing by setting up automatic transfers from your checking account or debit card each month. Then expect God to show up. Wait and see if the rest of your bills still get paid. Prayerfully ask yourself, "Do I have more trust in my savings account than I do in God?" My prayer for you, my friend, is that you will have more faith and less fear in your life when you learn that God really does take care of us, no matter what. He knows every detail regarding the circumstances of your life. Rest in the fact that God is in control.

Step 3

If tithing doesn't appear to fit into your current budget, please don't be dismayed. I challenge you to try it anyway. Most people who tithe will tell you, "I don't know how it happens—it just does. Bottom line—tithing has less to do with my money and more to do with my faith."

Kings and Priests

Have you ever heard of the difference between a king and a priest in God's economy? In my younger adult years, I somehow felt "lesser than" or "insignificant" compared to my family members who were dedicating their entire lives to full-time ministry. Then one day I read David R. High's book, *Kings and Priests*. That one book changed my focus and helped me identify what God was calling me to do for his glory in my life. It was much different than what other members of my family had been called to do. All Christians cannot have pulpit ministries. If that were true, who would pay the bills? According to David R. High, the wisdom God used to structure Israel can help us in the New Testament church. Kings and priests are two very different callings and offices.

The role of priests in Israel was to provide vision:

- Responsible for hearing from God
- Offered sacrifices on behalf of the people
- Received offerings and tithes from the people
- Took care of the house of God
- Took care of the widows and orphans
- Cared for strangers
- Encouraged people before battles

The role of kings in Israel was to administer provision:

- Collected taxes
- Destroyed the enemies of God and took the spoils of war
- Paid tithes and offerings to the priests
- Governed the physical affairs of the nation[2]

If a king tried to do a priest's job, or vice versa, he suffered consequences from the Lord. The separation brought respect for both callings. My question for you is: Are you a king or a priest? Take some time and pray about this question. Once you know for sure what your calling is, it may change the trajectory of your future.

The church needs to remember that kings who provide for the needs of the church are as valuable as the priests who hear from God and deliver sermons from the pulpit. God's kingdom on earth will go through a radical change if we choose to honor and respect kings as much as we do priests. Teamwork between priests and kings will multiply God's blessings and the effectiveness of the church to meet more people with the gospel of Jesus Christ.

Invest in God's Kingdom

I want to encourage you to research and pray about what God is leading you to support in your local community, in your church, or across the globe. God can use each and every one of us, no matter how large or how small our gifts are. If you currently have limited resources, please don't be dismayed. You can still give of your time and a portion of your income. My charge to you is to *just take the next step*. If you've never given anything to anyone, start with a small tithe. If you're already tithing, consider giving more sacrificially. Be an investor in kingdom causes. Your family will be blessed, and through your tithes and offerings, generations will change for the better.

I often get asked about ways to have discernment on which organizations, beyond the local church, are being productive with the resources people donate and gift to them. Nonprofit organizations should be transparent with their financials records. For example, if a large majority of the organization's budget goes to administrative salaries, rather than the actual work of helping people, that may not be an organization you want to support financially. Please do your homework. I recommend an online resource called Charity Navigator located at: https://www.charitynavigator.org. I strongly recommend asking lots of questions before you make a decision regarding whom you will support financially, beyond your local church.

Friend, I really want to encourage you to support causes and ministries that you're passionate about. Personally, my family has a passion for prison ministry, pro-life movements, and micro-financing loans for women in impoverished countries. What needs and causes touch your heart or keep you awake at night? Take a moment and prayerfully ask God to show you where your financial resources will have the greatest impact for God's kingdom and the people who need your help. *We are called to be the hands and feet of Christ. We're not called to sit on the sidelines and wait for someone else to help our neighbor.*

Let's be brave and be the change this world needs. And as we give faithfully, prayerfully, and sacrificially, let's remember the wise words of Malachi, "'Bring the whole tithe into the storehouse, that there may be food in my house. Test me in this,' says the Lord Almighty, 'and see if I will not throw open the floodgates of heaven and pour out so much blessing that there will not be room enough to store it'" (Mal. 3:10).

CHAPTER 4

Do Not Borrow from Peter to Pay Paul

SECRET #4: THE FAITHFUL MANAGE DEBT CAREFULLY

Give to everyone what you owe them: If you owe taxes, pay taxes; if revenue, then revenue; if respect, then respect; if honor, then honor.

Romans 13:7

I was a banker for many years. We worried about our customers that were overextended on their credit cards, especially at Christmas or Hanukkah time, the season of gift giving. Some customers failed to adhere to a realistic budget when buying gifts for their friends and family members. It was pretty obvious by mid to late December that they were not going to be able to pay for all of the assorted gifts they purchased, often with credit cards. It's not uncommon for people to become irrational and emotional spenders during the holiday season.

We had a saying at the bank during the holidays that I still remember to this day. We used to tell people, "Make sure you pay your bills so Repo Santa doesn't show up at your house this year." Repo Santa is Bad Santa at his worst. Nobody wants a visit from that jolly old man. Instead of giving gifts to you and your family, his job is to take back all of your new loot that you couldn't afford. I have a vivid picture in my mind of Santa Claus gathering up all of the presents under a Christmas tree and taking them *back up* the chimney because the gifts had not been paid for.

What's the most common financial mistake that people make today? I bet you already know. It's not a new phenomenon. We're all inherently sinful and selfish by nature, so we want everything *now*. If we don't learn the concept of delayed gratification, or self-control, before we become adults, we can easily get into trouble financially. Secret number four is learning to manage debt carefully in order to move from fearful insecurity to confident control of your personal finances.

It used to be that having a credit card was a luxury or a rarity, but now most households have several of them. We can get exactly what we want today, regardless of whether or not we can actually afford it. If we're not careful, we can become overextended on credit cards—it's quite a slippery slope financially. Just like any sin, a little is fun. We all like new stuff because it's exciting to get new things. Current studies regarding brain research show how shopping activates key areas of the brain, making us feel better and boosting our mood, at least temporarily.[1] Gazing into a beautifully decorated holiday window or locating a hard-to-find toy taps into the brain's reward center, triggering the release of brain chemicals that give you a "shopping high." This is where the term "retail therapy" comes from. If you're aware of the way your brain responds to shopping, it can help you make sense of the highs and lows of impulse shopping, avoid buyer's remorse, and lower your risk for overspending. Shopping really can become addictive if you're not careful. Under a mountain of stuff and debt, you may end up somewhere you never intended.

The Bible does not say that debt is a sin. However, debt essentially enslaves us to the one who provides the loan. Just like anything else that can be addictive if abused, a little is okay but a lot is overwhelming. At the same time, in some situations going into debt is a wise move financially. Debt can be used to purchase an item that will eventually lead you to financial freedom. Examples of good debts are mortgages to purchase a home or loans to start a business that will provide income for your family. As long as money is being handled wisely and the debt payments are manageable, it's not sinful to take on debt. However, we're required to pay back what we borrow. It's very easy to take this lightly, but if we borrow it, the debt is our responsibility to pay back.

Obviously, in order to become financially independent, we have to save more money and spend less money, and taking out a loan is definitely an expense, especially if the interest rate on the loan is high. Learning to avoid consumer debt is a paradigm shift for those who have gotten into the habit of putting everything on a credit card.

There are various ways to obtain credit, or in other words, borrow money. You can obtain credit without any collateral, using credit cards or unsecured lines of credit, or you can get a secured loan that requires you to pledge some form of collateral. Let me explain the different types of lending options available today so you can be an informed consumer. I think it's useful to know what they are, who uses them, and how they may affect your financial security.

Credit Cards

Credit cards are non-collateralized, or unsecured, loans that allow the cardholder to borrow money on demand, usually at the point of sale, up to the maximum credit line he or she has available. The interest rate on credit cards averages from eighteen to twenty percent per year. There are three reasons credit cards are quite expensive if not used responsibly. First, the financial company providing the credit card might charge the cardholder an annual fee to have the privilege of borrowing money on demand. Second, credit card companies charge interest on the amount borrowed if the cardholder does not pay off their outstanding balance in full each month. Third, financial companies make a lot of money every month because they charge late fees if the cardholder forgets to make the monthly payment on time. It doesn't matter if your payment is only one day late. They still charge a late fee. In light of this, always verify what day your bill is due and make sure you don't miss the deadline.

Because credit cards are so easy to use, they can become a terrible temptation and financial snare to some people. If you find it difficult to pay your credit card balance in full each month, I advise you to cut up your credit card, work on paying off your current debt, and go to an all-cash system.

Some people keep credit cards for emergencies or international travel needs, but to avoid temptation, they will actually freeze the credit card in a block of ice! That way, if the temptation or legitimate need arises to use the credit card, they have to go through the trouble of defrosting it, literally, before they can use it. The frozen credit card is a deterrent that gives them time to consider whether or not the use of the credit card is a wise choice or not. *Friend, the takeaway here is to learn to control your spending, not let your spending control you.*

I want to advise you to do a self-evaluation of your spending habits. You're the only person in the world who knows whether or not you have self-control when it comes to the use of credit cards. Having credit cards easily accessible in your purse or wallet at all times, may or may not cause you to spend money irresponsibly.

I want to be honest with you and tell you that I personally use credit cards. This may seem counterintuitive coming from the author of a book about personal finances. I personally use them for convenience. I purchase a lot of items included in my monthly budget with a credit card. For example, I use credit cards to pay expenses related to my children's school, meal delivery services, and business expenses that require me to have a credit card to pay my bill online. I also enjoy the benefits of airline miles as rewards for every dollar I spend. This rewards program saves my family thousands of dollars in travel expenses each year. Traveling and seeing the world is one of our passions. We look for ways to make it as affordable as possible.

I also use credit cards because I've learned to be disciplined and pay them off every month. As a result, I never pay late fees or interest on my purchases. I know that anything I charge on my credit card has to be included in my monthly budget. This is nonnegotiable.

Take some time to reflect on this discussion about the use of credit cards. If you're married, please consider having an open and honest conversation with your spouse about your own credit card use. Communication and honesty are very important when discussing issues that can either "make you or break you" financially.

Unsecured Lines of Credit

Unsecured lines of credit are very similar to credit cards, but are issued by a bank. The interest rate is usually significantly cheaper than what credit card companies charge. If you do not use the line of credit to borrow any money, then you do not pay any interest to the bank. If a borrower has a very poor credit score, they are going to have a very difficult time obtaining this type of loan.

People typically take out an unsecured line of credit for business purposes, such as cash flow management needs. Most people do not use unsecured lines of credit for personal expenses. A typical reason for why a business owner would use a line of credit is to manage inventory needs. For example, a clothing boutique could use a line of credit to buy new clothes, accessories, jewelry, shoes, etc., so customers can come into their boutique to shop. They have to buy inventory in order to have something available to sell to customers. If they're purchasing their inventory with the line of credit, even with interest expense, for less money than they're selling it for, they will make a profit on their sales. Once the merchandise is sold to customers, the boutique owner should pay down the line of credit and keep their profits. That is how they make a living.

As long as a business owner is responsible and financially prudent when it comes to the use of a line of credit, this is a fine business practice. One thing to note is that most lines of credit are put into place for one year. I suggest paying down any amount you have outstanding as soon as funds are available. Your bank has the right to require you to pay in full your outstanding balance when the line of credit matures, typically after one year. Though in many cases, a bank will be happy to renew your line of credit for another year if you've proven that you're a responsible borrower.

Secured Notes

Secured notes are loans that require collateral, which is an asset that the borrower offers the lender to secure the loan. If the borrower doesn't pay the required debt service payments, then the lender has the right to take the collateral. This process is called "repossessing an asset."

This is also a type of loan that is usually used by a business owner. For example, a manufacturing business may have to make a very large investment in new equipment to keep up with their business needs. If they don't have enough cash on hand to pay for the new equipment, then they could go to a bank and ask for a secured note, which is another name for a loan, to help them purchase their new equipment.

The security of the bank is that they get the collateral if the loan is not repaid. In this case, the collateral is the new manufacturing equipment. If the business owner fails to make his debt payments, then the bank will come and take his new equipment away and sell it to someone else, so the bank can get their money back. Just like an unsecured line of credit, as long as a business owner is responsible and financially prudent when it comes to the use of a secured note, this is a fine business practice that's quite common.

Car Note

The term of a car loan is typically three to five years. The car the borrower purchased secures the loan. It is the bank's collateral. Since cars depreciate in value, please do not consider them an investment. Cars are simply a utilitarian expense that allows us to get from one place to another, such as work, school, etc. In most cities in our industrialized society, it's very difficult to get around if you don't own a car, unless you live in a place like New York City where public transportation is easily accesible.

I want to encourage you to save up your money in cash before you purchase a car so you pay as little as possible for your vehicle. If you cannot do this, then please be very frugal when purchasing a new car. Please don't take on a large monthly car payment for your dream car if it's going to put a huge financial burden on your family and your household budget. Remember friend, we're not entitled to fancy cars. As I often tell my clients, there's a big difference between needs and wants.

There is nothing wrong with purchasing a gently used vehicle that's in very good condition. It will save you a lot of money in the long run. Believe it or not, a car depreciates in value by approximately twenty percent on the first day it's ever driven out of the parking lot of a car dealership.[2] For a car that costs $30,000 brand new, it will only be worth $24,000 on day two of ownership. It's crazy, right? Friend, let someone else pay for that initial depreciation. Then you can enjoy a nice car for less money in the long run, because after all, it's an expense and not an investment.

Car Lease

One more thing I want to address is the difference between buying a car and leasing a car. The major difference is that a leased car is simply borrowed for the term of the lease, usually twenty-four to thirty-six months. A lease allows a customer to borrow the difference between the upfront cost of a car and its projected residual value at the end of the lease. The down side is, unlike a loan to purchase a car, the customer will never own the car, ever.

On the positive side, the car will always be covered under a warranty and in most cases the maintenance will be covered during the lease term as well. Leasing is attractive to people who don't drive a lot of miles, people who always want a relatively new car, and who don't mind always having a car payment. Leasing can also help a customer avoid a big down payment.

Other Vehicles Loans

There are other types of loans for boats, tractors, trailers, and so on. They're structured very similarly to car notes. If you're purchasing a vehicle for recreational purposes, I really cannot advise taking on this type of loan, as "toys" should be purchased with cash. However, if you're using a vehicle for your business—for example, a farmer buying a tractor—then this form of debt is acceptable as long as you're certain that the business can sustain the cost of the loan.

Mortgage

A mortgage is a loan used to purchase a home that is secured by the entire value of the home. Since 2010, interest rates for mortgages have been extremely low, around three to four percent. Low interest rates are not good for earning interest in a savings account, but they are very beneficial for borrowers.

The millennial generation may not realize how unusually low mortgage interest rates are today compared to the 1980s and 1970s, when they ranged from eight percent to thirteen percent, and even as high as sixteen to seventeen percent in 1981 and 1982.[3]

If used responsibly, a mortgage is known as "good debt." The loan allows the borrower to make an investment in real estate and purchase a home for their family. Plus, the interest on the mortgage is tax deductible up to a loan amount of $1,000,000.

Please be very careful of mortgage loans with unfavorable terms to the borrower. We call these predatory loans. One example is an Adjustable Rate Mortgage (ARM). "Amortization rate" sounds like a complex idea. However, it simply means the total number of months you have until the mortgage loan will be paid off in full. Normally, the amortization rate is thirty years (360 months) or fifteen years (180 months). For a traditional mortgage, the interest rate is fixed for the life of the loan. However, an ARM will still have a fifteen-year or thirty-year amortization schedule, but the interest rate will only be fixed for five, seven, or ten years. I see people get into trouble, especially with five and seven-year ARMs. People are often attracted to the initial low interest rate of an ARM because it decreases their monthly payments. However, if interest rates have risen significantly since you originally obtained the loan, the monthly mortgage payment can skyrocket overnight at the maturity date.

Another type of loan to be concerned about is a mortgage with a balloon payment. These also can get borrowers into trouble. A balloon payment mortgage does not fully amortize over the term of the note. There is a balance due at maturity of the loan called a balloon payment. The reason they are attractive is the monthly payments are initially much lower. This allows people to afford more expensive homes. However, when the loan matures, the balloon payment, or simply the remaining balance on your mortgage loan, is due in *full*. There is no problem if the borrower has enough cash to pay off the loan, or simply refinance the loan when it matures. However, what if you cannot afford to pay off the balance of the loan *or* get approved to refinance your loan? Then you're really in trouble. I will talk more about purchasing a home and what type and size of mortgage I recommend in chapter seven.

Home Equity Loan

A home equity loan is a loan that a borrower has access to if they have significant equity in their home. The terms are often very favorable. Just like a mortgage, the interest is tax deductible. People will take out home equity loans to make repairs on their home, pay for college, or pay off debt. The borrower is free to use the funds however they wish.

Historically, this type of loan got a lot of people into trouble when the housing market crashed around 2007. When house values had previously skyrocketed, people borrowed from their homes, thinking that their home would continue to increase in value. When housing prices unexpectedly dropped significantly, people with a traditional mortgage and a home equity loan ended up owing more money on their home than what it was worth. This is why banks foreclosed on many homes.

Home Equity Lines of Credit (HELOC)

Instead of a lump sum of cash, a Home Equity Line of Credit (HELOC) offers homeowners a line of credit with a very low interest rate. The line of credit is collateralized by the equity in the home. This works like a credit card in that you can use it as long as there is availability on the line of credit and pay it off as you wish. If you do not have any funds "drawn up" on the line of credit, then you do not owe the bank anything. Some people put these loans in place as a safety net for cash or liquidity emergencies. They don't plan to use the line of credit, but it's available if needed. However, please understand that I don't think a HELOC eliminates the need for a cash reserve fund.

Home Improvement Loan

A home improvement loan is similar to a home equity loan, but the proceeds can *only* be used to make repairs and renovations to your home. You will be asked to show receipts for work completed on your home. Most likely, the bank will come out to the house periodically for inspections during construction. One major benefit of a home improvement loan is that it can be refinanced and rolled into your traditional mortgage loan. In contrast, a home equity loan *cannot* be refinanced and rolled into a mortgage loan.

If possible, it's always best to pay cash for home renovations and repairs so you avoid adding more debt to your home. If you do take out a home improvement loan to make improvements and/or repairs to your home, please ensure the appraised value of your home after you make the improvements will be much more than the cost of the actual work you have done. This will help prevent you from being "under water" on your home, or simply, owing more than the home is worth.

Bridge Loan

A bridge loan allows homebuyers to purchase a new home without having yet sold their previous home. The main reason you would need a bridge loan is because you need to get the equity out of your existing home before it's sold, in order to have a down payment, or possibly pay cash in full, for your new home.

I don't believe bridge loans are a bad idea, *if and only if,* you can definitely afford both the debt service payment on your existing mortgage, if you have one, *and* your new bridge loan. This can be a very stressful situation if it's not managed properly. Honestly, it is a means to an end to allow people to purchase a new home before they sell their existing home. Sometimes there are extenuating circumstances in life when this just makes life simpler. A good example would be a young family expecting a child and wanting to move to a new home before their baby is born, but they have not actually sold their existing home. A bridge loan would allow the family to get settled into their new home before the fast-approaching deadline of the birth of their child. It would also allow them to sell their existing home for top dollar when they get the best offer, which can take a bit of time.

Student Loans

Student loans are used to pay for higher education expenses such as: college or university tuition, fees, books, as well as professional training and trade certificate courses (culinary, technical, etc.) at a non-degree-granting school. Student loans may also be used to cover living expenses while someone is a full-time student. Obviously, it's always best for families to be able to save for college expenses for their children and avoid debt altogether. However, this honestly is not a realistic goal for many families. As a result, student loans become a means to an end.

A student loan allows an individual to earn a college education and/or an advanced degree so that he or she can increase their lifetime earning potential by a large percentage. I do advise that the student take on the college debt, *not* their parents. Parents need to be saving for retirement rather than taking on college loans that they may not live long enough to be able to pay off.

There is a difference between private student loans and

government student loans. Please do your homework and due diligence to make sure you're signing up for student loans with the lowest interest rate possible. Also, please be cautious and don't take on student loan debt unless you're reasonably sure you can complete a degree.

Sallie Mae is one of the largest private student loan providers in the country. They encourage students and families to supplement their savings by exploring grants, scholarships, and federal and state student loans, and to consider the anticipated monthly payments on their total student loan debt, and their expected future earnings, before considering a private student loan.

Reverse Mortgage

A reverse mortgage, or Home Equity Conversion Mortgage (HECM), is a type of home loan for older homeowners (sixty-two years old or more) that allows them to continue to live in their home for the rest of their life, but access the equity in order to provide liquidity, or income, during retirement. The senior also becomes exempt from paying any remaining mortgage payments if they still owe money on their home, until they die, sell, or move out of the home. One thing to remember is the homeowner is still responsible for property taxes and homeowner's insurance.

A reverse mortgage can be both good and bad. If you or a loved one is considering this type of loan, please make sure it is the right decision. Here is a list of issues to consider when evaluating the pros and cons of a reverse mortgage:

- Make sure you continue to be the only titleholder on your home.
- Be sure your loan is insured through the FHA (Federal Housing Administration).
- You will accumulate debt on your home that will eventually

be deducted from the sales proceeds if you die, sell, or move out of the home. Interest rates on the loan balance can be high and should be carefully evaluated before signing up for this type of loan.

Healthy Habits

As you can see, there are a lot of different lending options available today. With the exception of a (reasonable) mortgage and (reasonable) student loans taken out by the students themselves (not their parents), I cannot really recommend taking on any other form of personal debt.

The debt that I'm always most concerned about my clients managing properly is credit card debt. It's the most expensive way to obtain debt and very easy to abuse. Based on an analysis of Federal Reserve statistics, the average US household credit card debt today stands at $15,863, counting only those households carrying debt. It's epidemic. If you use credit cards to borrow money to pay for things you cannot afford, and you do not pay the balance off in full each month, it will take you many years to get out of debt. The credit card companies will get richer while you struggle to get ahead financially.

Here are six healthy habits you can create to help you conquer your spending on debt.

Habit One

Make sure you have a realistic monthly budget. This helps you to remain focused on your spending habits. You know for sure what you can and cannot afford to buy each month.

Habit Two

Stop and think before you make a purchase. Often, it's a good idea to wait a few days after initially thinking about a purchase to determine if it's simply an impulse buy, or something that you, or your family, truly need and can afford.

Habit Three

Avoid the trap at many clothing and big-box retail stores where they invite you to open a credit card at the time of purchase in order to save ten percent. Having lots of miscellaneous credit cards is not good for your credit score, and it encourages you to overspend.

Habit Four

Have a line item in your monthly budget for miscellaneous purchases. I have many clients that keep cash for these types of scenarios. Once the cash is gone, you cannot make any more miscellaneous purchases until the following month.

Habit Five

Have a separate savings account for vacations. This is one of the major expenses that people put on credit cards because the vacation is not part of their regular monthly budget. You may enjoy that week at Disney World, but will spend the rest of the year paying off your credit card. This really steals the fun from a vacation.

Habit Six

Make it a policy that you will never cosign a loan, even for a family member. If something goes wrong and they are unable to pay, you will be on the hook for the loan. The Bible warns, "Do not be one who shakes hands in pledge or puts up security for debts; if you lack the means to pay, your very bed will be snatched from under you" (Prov. 22:26–27). Having such a policy in place will also make it easier for you to say no graciously: "I'm sorry, but I've made a policy never to cosign a loan, so I can't help you with that" or "I'm sorry, but the Bible warns against cosigning loans, so I can't do that." Trust me, saying no will preserve your relationship with a family member better than saying yes.

Money and Marriage

Managing your money can be trickier once you're married and have to negotiate differing money priorities and philosophies. Often one person will be the saver, while the other person will be the spender. But since money troubles are one of the biggest causes of conflict and even divorce, you need to address the topic of debt up front. If you're considering marriage, put your financial situation out on the table, and if you are deeply in debt, you need to be responsible and create an immediate action plan for tackling your personal debt.

If you're already married and face substantial debt, sit down with your spouse and have an honest conversation without shaming one another. Work together and come up with a plan to tackle your debt. As you work together and make progress toward financial freedom, the process will be rewarding and fruitful.

Finally, when talking about debt, I often get asked this simple question: "Emily, what is your best advice for handling debt?" Friend, take a deep breath and don't make any decisions about large purchases, or taking on debt, without first praying about it. Do not make a decision and then ask God to bless it. Pray first, and then take action as the Holy Spirit leads you. Remember, the faithful avoid debt whenever possible, and they only take on "good" debt that they are confident they can repay.

CHAPTER 5

Pay Yourself First

SECRET #5: THE FAITHFUL MAKE A SAVINGS PLAN

Dishonest money dwindles away,
but whoever gathers money little by
little makes it grow.

Proverbs 13:11

Frank P. Carvey (originally Francesco Carevic) was born on September 29, 1888, in the village of Selca, on the island of Brac. The island of Brac is just a short distance in the Adriatic Sea from Split, Yugoslavia. However, it wasn't Yugoslavia then, it was Austria-Hungary. Today it is called Croatia. Frank was the oldest of ten children.

Frank's family was very poor and there were many mouths to feed. In 1902, the family vineyard and olive trees didn't produce much to live on, so it was decided that Frank should come to America. He was thirteen years old when he left home. Eventually, he arrived by ship at Ellis Island in New York as a new, barely-fourteen-year-old, immigrant to the United States of America. His only mission after surviving the risky voyage to America was to find work to help support his family.

When Frank first arrived in America, he went to San Francisco to work for an uncle that had sponsored his trip to America. Frank's

77

uncle owned a restaurant. He provided Frank with a place to live and a job at the restaurant as a busboy. Frank was also able to eat at the restaurant where he worked so he did not spend any money on food. Frank saved almost every penny he earned as a busboy while working at his uncle's restaurant. That was his choice. He soon knew beyond a shadow of a doubt that he wanted to grow up and get married, have a family, and enjoy a better life in the United States of America. However, he never forgot his family in Yugoslavia. From the day he came to America, Frank assumed responsibility for his family. Still a child himself, he sent a part of every paycheck he received back to his family in Yugoslavia.

Before Frank was twenty years old, he left his uncle in San Francisco to go out on his own. He continued a lifetime of association with the food business: first as a waiter, then a railroad dining car steward, then owning his own restaurant, to finally managing Lakewood Country Club in Dallas for twenty-six years, until his retirement from there in 1947.

After he found his way to Texas in 1910, he also found Ella Johnson, of Swedish heritage, and they married. He was twenty-four years old when his first child, Dorothy, was born in 1913. Frank and his wife Ella then had two more children: Helen and Frank, Jr. This story is part of my heritage. Dorothy is my maternal grandmother. Had Frank not come to America as an immigrant in 1902, I would not exist. None of my maternal family would exist. He passed down a legacy to his children, grandchildren, and great-grandchildren that hard work was something to be proud of. He taught his family to save money, to make wise choices financially, and to always give back to those in need. His legacy has lived on well past his death at the age of ninety-four in November of 1982. I was just eight years old at the time of his death, but I still remember the lessons he taught my family.

The story has been told to my family that when Frank's father died and his mother was alone with six children still living at home that she had to support, she was forced to borrow money from a moneylender. This man asked her what she had to guarantee repayment of that loan. Her reply was, "I have money that comes from America every month." The man asked how she could be sure of that and she said, "You will see, you will see." And the money always came. And it continued to come, regularly. Even after his mother died, it came to his brothers and sisters that were left in Yugoslavia. During the hard, hard years between World War I and World War II, Frank's financial support meant life itself to his family on Brac. During World War II, when all of Europe was in such desperate circumstances, Frank sent care packages with flour, sugar, and other staples to the family. The food he sent literally kept them alive.

If my great-grandfather, Frank Carvey, could save money and help support his family as a fourteen-year-old immigrant, then you and I surely can save money as well!

Starting a Savings Plan

I often get asked how to begin a savings plan. The hardest part is starting. Just like my great-grandfather taught my family, you have to make a choice to save regularly. You need to automate your savings plan so that money comes out of your bank accounts, or paycheck, systematically every month. If you wait to save money until the end of the month, I promise you will never have anything left over to save. If you consider saving money each month to be optional, you will have a difficult time being successful. Saving has to be a serious commitment and nonnegotiable. Consider making a monthly tithe to God who owns all of your resources, and then immediately pay yourself *before* you pay any other bills or make any other purchases. You're your own biggest advocate for becoming financially independent. *If you want to move from fearful insecurity to confident control of your personal finances, you need to have a savings plan in place.*

People often procrastinate when starting a new savings plan. It falls into the same category as starting a new diet. You fear you're going to be restricted and miss out on the fun stuff. *Diet* and *save* are both considered to be ugly four-letter words. "Let's eat that last ice cream sundae today, and then I will start my new diet plan tomorrow." But then tomorrow comes and you get asked to go out to dinner for Mexican food. "Oh well, one more day won't hurt. Right?" And so tomorrow never comes. What you really need is a lifestyle change, not a temporary diet.

The same goes for starting a savings plan.

Friend, accept your new assignment and start moving forward. Don't think of saving money as a punishment. Think of saving money as a means to *freedom*. It's a disciplined choice you can make today to benefit yourself and your family tomorrow. *If you take control of your finances today, then you won't be a victim of them tomorrow.* Nobody is making you save money *or* spend irresponsibly. By saving regularly, you're choosing a better life for yourself.

This new lifestyle may require supernatural strength to take a positive step forward. There are several ways to gather the strength you will need. Spend time in God's Word and pray for wisdom, energy, and focus. You may also need to meet with someone you trust who will provide you with wise counsel and be a rational sounding board.

This may sound overly simple, but there are three main ways to save:

- Work more.
- Want less.
- Save more.

Work More

Working more does not just mean adding an extra shift to your already long workweek. However, some people who are heavily in debt may choose this strategy for a season until they get out of debt and get back on their feet. I promise you that you can do hard things if you know the extra work is only for a season and not forever. The long-term benefits will eventually outweigh your short-term fatigue.

What would happen if you started to think differently about the other four-letter word: *work*? Have you considered how to increase your income by doing something besides your regular day job, maybe something you're passionate about? Think outside of the employment box. We already discussed this idea in chapter two in regards to building up your cash reserve account. The same principles are applicable to saving above and beyond your short-term cash reserve needs. Working more is also about being intentional with your time, talent, and resources. Think about your unique gift set and what gives you great joy. How could you leverage your specific gifts and talents to improve your financial situation?

Are you an excellent cook or a great party planner? Are you an athlete that could earn extra money as a coach or referee? Are you good at needlepoint or monogramming? Can you use your skills to make specialty gifts and sell them for profit? The key is to determine which skills you have that are valuable to others. Then you have to research the appropriate amount to charge for your service or product. This will be a paradigm shift. You're going to trade your value and skills for someone else's money. When you use your gifts, you will find that work doesn't necessarily feel like *work*.

Have you completed your monthly budget worksheet at the end of chapter two? If not, this would be a very good time to complete that exercise. You really need to have a realistic budget for your expenses. We talked a lot about discretionary income and expenses in chapter two.

Discretionary Income = All Income Sources - All Expenses

By working more, you are increasing your discretionary income by increasing your total income stream.

Want Less

Now let's talk about ways to decrease your expenses. Are you spending money on things that have no long-term intrinsic value? If so, are you willing to make a choice today to simply want less? This is a personal question. I want to encourage you to take some time and pray about this one.

In the US, we've gotten into a habit of acquiring things first, and then figuring out how to pay for them later. That is why credit cards have become a problem for many people. The following statistics illustrate just how much people are using credit cards these days:

- Average debt per credit card that usually carries a balance: $7,527.
- Average debt per credit card that does *not* usually carry a balance: $1,154.
- Total US outstanding consumer debt: $3.62 trillion as of May 2016.[1]
- Average APR on a credit card with a balance on it: 15.18% in Q4, 2016.[2]

We are buying things we cannot afford. Are you personally enslaved to credit cards? Are you worried about status symbols and trying to appear wealthy? Are you trying to keep up financially with other friends in your community, but struggling to do so? If so, you may need to face up to your "keep up with the Joneses" mentality and think about how it's hurting you. Learning to be content with what you have doesn't cost anything except a bit of humility.

One way to want less is to clearly identify the next discretionary purchase that fits your values and interests, advances your goals, and brings you the greatest satisfaction. The more you are aiming toward what you really need and want, the more you'll be able to refrain from spending on things that don't matter as much to you. For example, a child might refrain from buying candy in order to save up for a new LEGO set. A student might refrain from buying clothes or going to concerts in order to save money to buy a car. A young couple might forgo vacations and eating out in order to save for a home. Another person might choose to drive late-model cars in order to spend money on a kitchen renovation instead. This tactic works not only on the big purchases, but also on the little ones. Do you get more joy from your daily cup of Starbucks than from a weekly night out at a restaurant? Then drink the coffee and skip the dinner! One great way to spend less is to spend mindfully, on things and experiences you really care about and genuinely enjoy.

Finally, you might want to ask yourself: Am I trying to fill a deep-seated need in my life by overspending on stuff or splurging on experiences? Friend, there will never ever be enough new stuff or exciting events to satisfy you. Only God can satisfy your needs for love and self-worth. God has placed an emptiness in your soul that can only be filled by him. Nothing money can buy will ever fill that emptiness. You may experience temporary happiness, but never lasting joy. Stuff will always rust, fade, break, go out of style, or become obsolete. Travel, concerts, plays, gourmet meals, and all the other activities you brag about on social media will eventually fade from your memory. Will you commit today to ask God for more of him and less of the stuff of this world? I want to encourage you to switch your focus from looking outward at the world and its trappings, to looking upward toward a God who loves you very much. Ultimately, you will find much more peace and lasting joy.

Remember, "Keep your lives free from the love of money and be content with what you have, because God has said, 'Never will I leave you; never will I forsake you'" (Heb. 13:5).

Save More

Changing your focus on a day-to-day basis may sound wonderful in theory, but can be hard to implement. The first practical step you can take today is to make the choice to save more instead of spend more. The very stuff you're consuming to fill yourself up may be the actual underlying cause of your anxiety. That's something to think about, huh?

If you will focus more on saving, and less on spending, you will experience financial freedom. Saving instead of spending will calm your spirit emotionally. You will rest easier at night knowing that you're helping yourself financially, rather than hurting yourself. This is what Jesus wants for all of us. He wants us to find peace and rest. Pray about your spending habits and ask God to reveal areas in your life where you're not being responsible with the money he has provided for you.

The second step is to categorize the items and services in your life that are truly needs as opposed to wants. Wanting less leads to spending less money, which will ultimately allow you to save more. Don't delay the process. Start saving money as soon as you can. The younger you are when you start saving money systematically every month, the longer your money will be able to grow and take advantage of compound interest. I have found that most people can save more money each month just by being intentional about how they are spending their income.

The third step is to find ways to spend less on needed expenses without compromising the quality of a product or service. For example, shop around for lower rates on insurance costs, such as car insurance or homeowner's insurance. Also, please pay attention to current mortgage interest rates to determine whether or not you're eligible to refinance your home and save even more money, every single month.

Also, take some time to evaluate what you're currently paying for services such as internet, cable, and monthly cell phone services. Often companies will bundle these expenses if you use one provider. It may be possible to save a considerable amount of money each month and receive the exact same quality of service. It just takes some time and effort on your part to do your homework.

Another tip I've learned from some of my friends is how to be a savvy coupon collector. Unfortunately, I also see people buying things they really don't need just because they have a coupon. *That is not how you save money!* However, if you need liquid laundry detergent and you have a coupon for that exact product, by all means, use the coupon! Another idea is to purchase generic or store brand items when grocery shopping. Often the products are exactly the same as the name brand item but they are less expensive. Once again, you will not sacrifice quality, but still save money.

The fourth step is to pay yourself first. Automate, automate, automate. Consider setting up an automatic draft from your checking account every single month on a specific day. Allocate a fixed amount to a savings or brokerage account. If you have an adequate cash reserve already, start investing to grow your assets. Your age, resources, and stage of life will determine what your savings goals should be focused on.

In terms of savings, let's discuss what your goals and objectives should be for each decade of your adult life prior to retirement. Remember, if you have a big goal to focus on, that will help you to resist the urge to splurge on the little things.

Twenties

Your finances are most likely a lot simpler now than they will be in the future, when you may be juggling priorities like saving for a down payment on a house, while also starting a family. Your twenties are an ideal time to establish good money habits that can help carry you through the next decades. I'm often asked if new college graduates should pay off credit card debt or student loans before they start saving for the future. My answer is: Yes. Always be proactive with paying off debt. However, split your discretionary income each month between debt service and savings, working on both goals simultaneously. Time is on your side. You have many years ahead of you to benefit from compound interest. In your twenties, your life is a marathon, not a sprint.

Your first savings goal should be a cash reserve equal to at least three months' worth of living expenses for emergencies (see chapter two). As soon as you have a cash reserve account funded, start saving for retirement, even if you still have some debt to pay off. The earlier you start saving for retirement, the sooner you will achieve financial freedom (we will talk more about the wonders of compound interest in chapter eight). Then you will have options on how to spend your time. In other words, you can choose to travel, volunteer, or spend more time with your family. Trust me, the benefit of compound interest is something you don't want to miss out on in your twenties. Plan to monitor your accounts and goals at least once per year. Life will happen. Over time, you may need to make adjustments to your savings plan.

If you have a company-sponsored retirement plan such as a 401(k), make sure you're contributing the maximum allowable contribution that you can afford, especially if your employer provides a match of a certain percentage of your income. The maximum allowable personal contribution changes every year. In 2017, the maximum personal contribution was $18,000. If an employee is over age 50, they are also allowed to contribute an additional $6,000 as a catch-up provision for a total of $24,000. Any matching funds your employer contributes to your personal retirement plan is free money to you. The employer's contribution is in addition to the $18,000 to $24,000 that you are allowed to contribute. Remember, contributions to retirement plans are tax deductible.

Thirties

The financial decisions you made in your twenties, and the decisions you will make in your thirties, will have a large impact on your forties, fifties, and beyond. During this decade, your financial goals are likely to get a bit more complicated. Many people are still paying off credit card debt and student loans, working on building emergency savings, and kicking retirement savings into high gear—while also buying a home and starting a family. This is why it's so important to gain focus and be more prudent with your finances in your thirties. Make sure you keep a close eye on your budget so you can set up realistic savings goals for yourself and your family.

Big life events like getting married, having kids, or buying a house are important times to assess whether your insurance needs are being appropriately met. If you have children, securing term life insurance now will help them maintain financial security in the future if anything should happen to you (see chapter six for more on insurance). In addition, you'll probably have to plan for childcare costs, as well as starting to save for college. For the latter, consider opening a 529 plan and contributing what you can now to help defray tuition costs and other college fees down the road (more on that in chapter nine).

Forties

At this point in your life, you definitely want to be out of the credit card debt-cycle and have any student loans paid off. As your income increases, don't forget to keep a cash reserve, and make sure that it reflects your current income. Also, be sure to revisit your retirement projections, while also paying attention to other ways to invest and grow your money (see chapter eight).

If you have kids, you may be feeling the need to put your retirement savings on hold in favor of saving for college tuition.

Please don't let guilt lead you to make poor financial decisions. *Remember, your kids can work or borrow money for college if necessary, but you cannot borrow money for retirement.*

Although you may not have paid much attention to your investment portfolio in your thirties, you may have started accumulating some wealth by your forties. These are typically your high income earning years, which makes it a good time to become more thoughtful about whether you're investing in the right way.

Fifties

A lot of events happen in your fifties: looking ahead to retirement, kids may go off to college, mortgage payments, and portfolio management. This stage of life is when you really need to be proactive with financial planning. Continue to revisit your savings and investment goals often. Now is the time to fully prepare for retirement, whether it's five years away or twenty years away.

At this point, try to save as aggressively as possible. Focus on reducing the risk in your investment portfolios, which can be accomplished by reducing stock holdings and increasing the percentage of bonds. Traditionally, stocks are considered more volatile than bonds. As you get closer to retirement, your emergency savings goal should now be one to two years of cash. The fifties can be the sandwich generation years. You may need to be supporting your kids while also taking care of aging parents. However, stay focused on your personal financial goals.

Consider the parameters of supporting your grown children financially. If you paid for every expense when your children were minors, proactively consider whether you will continue to contribute to your young adult's expenses, like a down payment for a home or graduate school tuition. This is not a decision to be made hastily, because it may have long-term effects on your personal retirement goals.

I have observed that many pre-retirees underestimate their

future financial retirement needs, while also overestimating their current financial position. This is exactly why I want to encourage you to seek wise counsel and have a person you're accountable to, such as a financial advisor or another person you trust.

I also suggest utilizing online calculators to determine how much you need to save in order to maintain your standard of living while in retirement. The math will not lie. The calculations will either confirm you're on the right track, or allow you to adjust your expectations for saving for retirement.

Friend, regardless of which stage of life you're currently in, I want to strongly encourage you to begin a savings plan if you haven't already done so. *It's never too late to start saving!* Then continue to monitor your goals and savings needs throughout each decade of your life. Systematic savings plans will make all the difference in your stress level related to your finances. Please remember: The faithful make a savings plan to move from fearful insecurity to confident control of their personal finances!

Is Your Life Insured?

SECRET #6: THE FAITHFUL INSURE THEMSELVES AGAINST DISASTER

> *The blameless spend their days under*
> *the LORD's care,*
> *and their inheritance will endure*
> *forever.*
> *In times of disaster they will not wither;*
> *in days of famine they will enjoy plenty.*
>
> Psalm 37:18–19

A few years ago, my husband's beloved grandmother passed away at the age of eighty-seven. She had suffered with Alzheimer's disease for several years, so her body began to fail her rapidly. She had lived a very fruitful life, and it was a blessing that now she was with her Savior. She had a close, personal relationship with Jesus throughout her entire life. Her family and friends were at peace knowing that she would spend eternity with her heavenly Father. There was no doubt or fear associated with death for her. She knew beyond a shadow of a doubt that her eternal life was, in fact, insured.

In order to honor my husband and his family, I volunteered to write and read aloud her eulogy at her funeral. Honestly, eulogies are not a part of my normal speaking engagements. I talk to groups about financial planning, money management, or types of insurance like we will discuss in this chapter. Preparing her eulogy with much prayer and thought was a very poignant moment for me. I stopped to think about my own life. They say the best way to live is to write your own eulogy, and then live backward in order to live your life with great focus and purpose. I began to ask myself the following questions:

- How am I spending my days here on earth?
- Am I blessing others?
- Am I using my time and talents well?
- Am I serving God to further his kingdom?

As I wrote her eulogy and tried to summarize the highlights of her life in a fifteen-to-twenty-minute speech, I had the very sobering thought that our time here on earth is in fact quite short.

Friend, the hard reality is that your life too will eventually end. Dying is something you can count on. The most important question you need to answer is whether or not your eternal life is insured. I want you to know beyond a shadow of a doubt that you will spend eternity with your heavenly Father. There are no strategies or good deeds that will get you there. The only way to have eternal life is a relationship with Jesus Christ. If you ignore everything else in this book, please do not ignore the gospel of Jesus Christ and the eternal hope that is found in him alone. "For God so loved the world that he gave his one and only Son, that whoever believes in him shall not perish but have eternal life" (John 3:16).

Who Depends on You?

I want to make myself very clear. The insurance question I am most concerned about is your *eternal* life insurance. However, your children and dependents are also very important. One of the most loving things you can do for your family is to provide for them financially when you pass away. Life insurance is designed to protect family members from severe financial strain at the exact time that they are grieving from the loss of a family member. If you are financially responsible for any dependents, you need to protect their future if something unforeseen happens to you.

A common mistake I see couples make frequently is that they assume they don't need life insurance on a spouse that doesn't work outside the home. Don't underestimate the value of the time and service this person provides for your family just because he or she doesn't collect a traditional paycheck. If you sat down to calculate how much it would cost to outsource the following services for your family, I think you would be quite shocked:

- Personal assistant to run errands and do laundry
- Culinary chef to grocery shop and prepare all meals
- Full-time nanny to take care of the children when the other spouse is working full time
- A chauffeur to carpool kids to and from activities

It would be quite expensive to pay all of the service providers you would need to replace your spouse who doesn't work outside of the home. Please don't forget to insure the spouse who helps keep your home running smoothly, and most important, makes sure your children are well taken care of. There are many types of life insurance that can be purchased. Life insurance provides either a lump sum of cash, or an ongoing income stream for a policyholder's family, if he or she suddenly dies. A life insurance settlement can be used for any number of purposes, such as:

- Replacement of your income
- Coverage of funeral expenses
- Payment of any outstanding medical bills

- Elimination of other debts, such as credit card debt, car payments, or student loans
- Elimination of mortgage debt so your loved ones can own a home free and clear
- Coverage of any potential estate tax liability
- Payment for a college education for your children or grandchildren
- Savings for the remaining spouse's retirement

In order to make an informed decision before purchasing a new policy or contract, you need to understand what you're buying. Sadly, some insurance agents are only concerned with selling a product in order to make a commission. Always do your due diligence on the person from whom you are buying life insurance.

The most popular life insurance product available today is term life insurance. Typically, it's quite inexpensive. However, it may or may not be the best choice for your particular situation. This is why you always need to seek wise counsel. Let's discuss the different types of life insurance products available today, and how to determine the amount of life insurance your family needs. One size does not fit all.

Term Life Insurance

Term life insurance, or term assurance, is life insurance that provides coverage at a fixed rate of payment for a limited period of time—usually ten, twenty, or a maximum of thirty years. After the term of the policy expires, coverage at the previous rate of premiums is no longer guaranteed. The policyholder must then decide whether or not they still need life insurance. At that time, they can either forgo coverage or obtain new coverage with different payments or conditions. If the person who is insured dies during the term of the policy, the death benefit will be paid to his or her beneficiary. A little-known fact about all life insurance policies is that the death benefit is paid to the beneficiaries of the policy tax-free. This is quite an attractive feature of life insurance.

Permanent Life Insurance Policies

Permanent life insurance policies include: whole life, universal life, variable life, and variable universal life, which guarantee coverage at fixed premiums for the lifetime of the covered individual. Coverage stays in force indefinitely, as long as the insurance premiums are paid.

Preservation of money and stable investment returns are two reasons that permanent insurance policies are popular with high-income individuals. A portion of each premium paid goes into a cash-value account, or an investment account, depending on the type of policy. The funds inside of the life insurance policy grow on a tax-deferred basis. My clients have accessed cash inside permanent insurance policies to supplement college savings needs, pay for health care expenses or other emergencies, add to retirement savings, or invest in real estate. My clients like the fact that they are in control of how they use the cash inside of their insurance policy. Another benefit of permanent insurance is that the cash inside of the policy is protected from creditors in the event of a lawsuit. There are various types of permanent insurance policies, and they all come with different durations, structures, costs, and variations.

Whole Life Insurance

Whole life insurance coverage offers guaranteed insurance for the duration of the policyholder's life. Such policies include a tax-deferred cash value that increases until the contract has been surrendered. Premiums for whole life insurance policies remain unchanged, and the policyholder has a guaranteed death benefit.

I recommend this type of insurance when a person wants to lock in their premiums and insurability, from a medical standpoint, for their entire lifetime. If your health dramatically changes in unexpected ways, and you only have a term life insurance policy, you may not be insurable after your term policy matures. The reality is that you're never going to be younger than you are today. Your age and your health are the two primary factors that affect your ability to purchase life insurance to protect your loved ones if you pass away unexpectedly.

Another benefit of this type of insurance is to save cash inside of your life insurance policy. You can take a nontaxable loan from yourself from the cash value inside of your policy if you ever have a liquidity need. In addition, the cash inside of a life insurance policy is protected from creditors from a legal standpoint. This is particularly attractive to those who are worried about being sued for business or personal reasons.

Universal Life Insurance

Universal life insurance is much like whole life insurance, except that the protection, premiums, and cash value can all be adjusted during the term of the contract. The cash values also accrue interest at a rate set by the insurance company. This type of insurance is useful for folks who want to save as much money as possible that is protected from creditors and litigation.

Variable Life Insurance

Variable life insurance policies combine aspects of an investment fund with a whole life insurance policy. A general account acts as the insurance company's liability account, which determines the death benefit, or surrender value, of the insurance policy. A separate account is composed of several investment funds from the insurance provider's portfolio. The policy is called a variable life insurance policy because the overall death benefit and value of the cash can change. The advantage of this type of insurance is upside growth potential for the funds invested inside of the life insurance policy, while still providing protection from creditors and litigation.

Variable Universal Life Insurance

Similar to a Variable Life Insurance policy, Variable Universal Life Insurance (often shortened to VUL) is a type of life insurance that builds cash value inside of the policy. The benefit of a VUL is the fact that the cash value can be invested in a wide variety of separate accounts, similar to mutual funds, and the choice of which of the available separate accounts to use is entirely up to the contract owner.

How Much Insurance Do I Need?

One of the questions I am often asked is, "How much life insurance do I need to protect my family?" There is a way to calculate how much life insurance you really need to safely cover the financial needs of your dependents. This is a resource I'm sharing at the end of this chapter for free. I often use this spreadsheet with my clients in my financial planning practice. My sincere desire is that you can utilize this tool to make a wise decision regarding the purchase of life insurance for your family. Trust me, you don't want to be under-insured, or pay too much in premiums and be over-insured.

Life insurance is an important part of your overall financial plan. Don't underestimate its value. It can help provide financial security if you unexpectedly pass away when you still have family members who are dependent on you to help provide for their needs. It's a gift to provide financial security to your loved ones, whether you're alive or not. Consider taking action today to determine whether or not you have enough insurance to support your loved ones. If you need to apply for more coverage, don't delay! The future is not certain.

Besides life insurance, there is another form of insurance that is critical to assuring your financial security. It's called disability insurance. To illustrate the need for this very important, but often overlooked insurance, let me tell you a true story.

Trent's Story

I recently had the privilege of getting to know a new friend named Trent. Honestly, his story is quite tragic. However, he has inspired me to count my blessings. Trent learned that he had no choice but to fully rely on God for his daily needs. I now believe that his dependency on God for his daily provision is a healthier attitude than falsely believing that we are in control and that the weight of the world is on our shoulders.

Trent and his family would have been completely devastated financially if he had not purchased long-term disability insurance before becoming paralyzed as a result of a rare autoimmune disorder. Trent's testimony is told best in his own words.

> Emily,
>
> Thank you for the opportunity to tell my story. I hope it encourages your readers to purchase long-term disability insurance. It's a very small price to pay to protect your family from being poverty stricken after an unforeseen illness or injury.
>
> After we got married, my wife and I lived in West Palm, Florida, for about ten years. I worked in a management position and my wife worked as a teacher. From the beginning of my career, I always purchased the Cadillac of insurance plans for my health coverage. This also included any supplemental benefits that my company offered.

My employer offered short-term disability insurance paid by the company. Most important, I also had the option to purchase long-term disability insurance. Believe it or not, the after-tax cost of my long-term disability insurance was only $1.61 per month. The insurance guaranteed sixty percent of my income if I ever became permanently disabled. Since I paid my portion of the required insurance premiums after tax, the benefits could not be taxed twice. As a result, my benefits would be tax free should I ever need them.

Honestly, I never thought I would need to use my short-term or long-term disability insurance benefits. However, since the cost of the monthly premiums was less than the average cost of a cup of coffee, I decided it was a wise financial move to apply for disability coverage.

We always planned for my wife, Nicole, to work as a teacher until we had children. Then she would be a stay-at-home mom and homeschool our children. However, God had a different plan. Nicole became pregnant with twins in 2010. Unfortunately, she experienced a very difficult pregnancy and our twins were born prematurely in May of 2011. As a result, both of our babies had a lot of medical complications. Some of the medical expenses necessary to keep them alive in the NICU were not completely covered by our health insurance. We quickly drained our savings to pay for our children's healthcare needs. Eventually, our twins were healthy enough to leave the hospital and come home in July of 2011. We were so grateful that our babies were alive and healthy. We were looking forward to getting back on our feet financially and starting our lives as a family of four. Believe it or not, I broke my ankle the day after we brought the twins home from the hospital for the first time. I had to have surgery and be on short-term disability until I recovered.

Then, on December 16, 2011, I unexpectedly became paralyzed by a very rare autoimmune condition called Guillain-Barre Syndrome. It came on very fast. Due to an error in the paperwork from the ER to the ICU, I was not treated with the correct medicine that could have given me back full mobility. Since I had taken so much time off of work when our twins were in the NICU, I had no more paid vacation. I had also used up my short-term disability benefits when I broke my ankle. I immediately went onto long-term disability. I spent a month and a half in a hospital rehabilitation treatment center. Thank goodness I had disability insurance to provide some income for our family.

After seeing some improvement in my condition and moving back to Texas in April of 2012, I started to decline again. Specialists then diagnosed me with a progressive form of CIDP (chronic inflammatory demyelinating polyneuropathy). Our health care costs continued to grow. I needed constant physical therapy as well as ongoing medical treatments. Nicole went back to work as a teacher and our twins were put into daycare.

However, God did not forget us nor forsake us. He answered our prayers for funds to sustain our family. My employer found a small pension that I didn't even know existed. The pension gave us a small amount of money that allowed us to rent a home. We continued to pray and reach out to those who would pray with us and provide emotional support and friendship. We were blessed again when our friends raised money to help sustain us financially. We even received money to purchase a wheelchair lift to accommodate a van so that I could drive.

I believe that we are all naturally people who dream about tomorrow. We want to work and provide for our families, and then eventually retire. However, our paradigm has completely shifted. We now have new dreams; ones that have adapted to our new normal and with God as our leader. God was with me when I decided to pay that small $1.61 premium for disability insurance. Without that decision, we would have no home and be dependent on social services. Instead, we have a roof over our heads, a car to get to church, and my wife has a job. As I am writing this letter, we are sitting on the sofa with our beautiful, four-year-old twins.

God is good.

Trent

The Importance of Disability Insurance

Trent's story may seem like an outlier, but did you know that during the course of your career, you're much more likely to become disabled and need disability insurance than you are to die and need life insurance? According to the US Census Bureau, nearly 1 in 5 Americans has a disability.[1] If you're not able to work because of health issues, you should have a backup plan to cover your monthly fixed expenses, as well as your medical care. I want to encourage you to stop and ask yourself the following question: "If I get sick or injured and can no longer work, will I be able to pay my bills and maintain my current standard of living?" If the answer to this question is no, please don't get discouraged. There are practical ways to plan for a disability from a financial standpoint.

How Much Do You Know about Disability Insurance?

You probably don't hesitate to insure assets such as your house or automobile, but you may not have coverage for another valuable asset: your ability to generate income. Believe it or not, your ability to go to work and provide a living to support yourself and/or your family is your most valuable asset. When consumers were asked questions about disability insurance in a LIMRA (Life Insurance and Market Research Association) survey, only four percent demonstrated a high level of knowledge. Therefore, I feel it's very important to educate you, my reader friend, on the purpose and importance of disability insurance.

The odds that an American entering the workforce today will become disabled before retiring are one in three. You may be surprised to learn that only nine percent of disabilities are caused by catastrophic events, such as a serious accident or injury. The main cause of disability in the United States is related to common illnesses and chronic medical conditions, such as back pain and arthritis. However, only about twenty-nine percent of American workers have some form of disability insurance.[2]

A disability income insurance policy could replace a percentage of your income (up to the policy limits) if you're unable to work as a result of an injury or illness. Benefits may be paid for a specified number of years, or until you reach retirement age. Some policies may pay benefits if you cannot work in your current occupation; others may pay only if you cannot work in any type of job.

If you or a loved one ever becomes disabled, please remember that God can use affliction and physical disabilities for our good, even though the process may be extremely painful. Remember what the apostle Paul wrote about his own affliction, "Therefore, in order to keep me from becoming conceited, I was given a thorn in my flesh, a messenger of Satan, to torment me. Three times I pleaded with the Lord to take it away from me. But he said to me, 'My grace is sufficient for you, for my power is made perfect in weakness.' Therefore I will boast all the more gladly about my weaknesses, so that Christ's power may rest on me. That is why, for Christ's sake, I delight in weaknesses, in insults, in hardships, in persecutions, in difficulties. For when I am weak, then I am strong" (2 Cor. 12:7–10).

In my experience, I have never met anyone who thought they were going to have a car accident, become paralyzed, or find out that they have cancer before the day that it happened. When the accident occurred, or the doctor called with the diagnosis, everything in their life changed in an instant. Time stood still. Questions came at lightning speed.

- What does this mean for me?
- Will I live? If I do live, will I be miserable physically?
- Who will pay for my health care needs if I cannot work?
- Who will take care of my kids?
- I don't want to be a burden to my family. How am I going to survive?

Advice for Purchasing Disability Insurance

For most of my clients, I recommend carrying enough personal disability insurance to replace at least sixty percent of your earnings should you ever become disabled. If you are a married couple and you depend on both of your incomes to maintain your standard of living, you should both carry disability insurance. *Your ability to generate income is one of your most valuable resources. Please do not forget to insure it.*

There are two types of personal disability insurance: short-term and long-term disability insurance. The major difference pertains to the length of coverage and the percentage of your income the insurance will replace if you become eligible for benefits.

Typically, short-term disability insurance will replace forty to sixty percent of your weekly salary. Short-term disability coverage usually begins anywhere from one to fourteen days after an employee becomes ill, or has an injury that makes them unable to work. Coverage of benefits may vary from nine to fifty-two weeks from eligibility. Every plan has its own provisions so make sure you understand your specific benefits. If your employer provides your short-term disability insurance, the company may require their employees to use sick days before collecting short-term disability benefits. It is also pretty common for people to use short-term disability benefits for maternity coverage for up to ninety days.

Many insurance companies limit long-term disability benefits to between fifty percent and eighty percent from all sources of disability income, prior to the disability. For example, if you also qualify for Social Security disability benefits, those payments you receive could be deducted from your benefit amount from your own insurance policy. Some individual policies will pay you partial benefits if you can only work part time as a result of sickness or an injury. Individual policies specify how much you will be paid, how soon after you are disabled that benefits will begin, and when benefits will end.

If you do become disabled and are covered by insurance, the monthly benefits will be payable for a fixed period of time. Your specific benefits will always be outlined in your policy contract. The most common benefit periods for long-term disability insurance are: two years, five years, to age sixty-five or for the rest of your life, while disability continues. The longer your insurance will pay you benefits, the higher the premiums will cost. One strategy for reducing the cost of a long-term disability insurance policy is to extend the waiting period, which is the time between when the disability occurs and when you start receiving benefits. Choosing a 90-day or 180-day waiting period (instead of thirty days) may help lower your premium cost. There are two additional features of disability income policies that I want you to understand. The terms can be confusing.

- Non-cancelable protection means that your insurance policy's premium can never be raised above the amount shown in the policy, and benefits may not be reduced, as long as the premiums for the policy are paid on time.

- Guaranteed renewable is a feature that gives the owner of the policy the right to renew his or her policy, with the same benefits, but the insurer can increase your premiums. The insurance company can only raise premiums for coverage if they are increasing the premiums for all other policyholders in the same class (i.e., having the same characteristics).

There are also many riders, or optional benefits, you can now purchase when buying personal disability insurance. I want you to be an informed consumer, so I have outlined the most common disability insurance riders available today, along with my recommendations.

Future Purchase Option (Guaranteed Insurability Option)

The future purchase option allows the insured to buy more disability income insurance if his or her income increases, without providing proof of medical insurability. In other words, the owner of the policy never has to have a medical exam or physical again. Even if you develop a medical condition that would normally prevent you from obtaining additional coverage, you could still increase your benefits if you have proof that your income has increased. I recommend this rider for folks who are in the early to mid stages of their career and expect their income to continue to increase annually.

Cost-of-Living Adjustments (COLA)

Cost-of-Living Adjustments provide an annual increase in benefits. The percentage of increase is usually based on a consumer price index, or a predetermined percentage, such as three percent or five percent annually. This is a very important feature. A COLA allows your benefits to increase annually in order to keep pace with inflation. I recommend this rider to all of my clients because it's so important.

Residual Benefit

A residual benefit pays the insured a portion of the monthly disability benefit if he or she has a reduction in income due to a disability. In most cases, this happens when the owner of the policy has gone back to work, but is only able to work part time. Ordinarily, the insured must satisfy a minimum percentage loss in earnings to qualify. I recommend this rider to individuals who even if they are disabled, could work in some capacity. For example, a physician, surgeon, or dentist who loses a finger, or has a hand injury, may not still be able to practice their medical specialty on patients, but they could still be a university professor. This rider would supplement the reduction in pay that they would have as a result of an injury.

Social Security Rider

The Social Security rider pays you a benefit even if you're not able to receive Social Security disability benefits because of the Social Security Administration's definition of disability. Unless the rider is very inexpensive, I do not usually recommend purchasing this rider.

Protection from Disaster

Please remember that all types of insurance are designed to protect the owner of the policy from the worst-case scenario. My sincere hope is that you'll never need to use disability income insurance in your lifetime. That is the best-case scenario. However, as we all know, there are no guarantees in life. That is why insurance was invented. It protects you and your family from financial ruin if you become sick, injured, or die while you still have financial responsibilities to support your loved ones.

Friend, please consider purchasing long-term disability insurance, either through your employer, or as an individual policy.

Group benefit policies are usually less expensive if you have access to disability coverage through your employer. However, if you leave your current job, most likely you won't be able to take your insurance with you. Another option is to purchase an individual disability policy from an insurance agent. It may be more expensive than group coverage, but you own the policy as long as you continue to pay the premiums. It doesn't matter if you change jobs, as long as you're in the same occupation. Be advised, however, that if you're employed in a more dangerous occupation, your premiums will be higher than if you're an office worker.

I sincerely believe that if you can afford it, the premiums for long-term disability insurance are worth the peace of mind that it will give you and your family. You'll be able to rest in the knowledge that if something unforeseen happens to you medically during your prime working years, you won't also be devastated financially. If you're still questioning whether this is a good investment, let me remind you that it's not an investment. It's insurance. That is why you should consult a knowledgeable professional that can assist you in purchasing the best possible insurance for the lowest premium dollars.

Now let's take a look at another important and often overlooked type of insurance.

Long-Term Care Insurance

I am personally in the life stage called *the sandwich*. That means that I have both aging parents and young children at the same time. My parents are now in their seventies, and I'm over F-O-R-T-Y years old. It honestly is very difficult for me to believe. I have no idea how it happened. Then I glance at a mirror and realize I need to pluck a gray hair out of the crown of my head. If the sun is shining just right, I can clearly see all of my newly acquired "sparkles."

My children are still young because I had my first child when I was almost thirty-two years old. I'm the mother of an eleven-year-old daughter and a seven-year-old son. My plate is rather full. If you find yourself in the sandwich stage of life, it can be quite a challenge, both financially and emotionally, if you and your family are not properly prepared.

In the year 2000, I worked as a private banker for JP Morgan Chase in Dallas. I provided financial planning and investment management advice to high net worth individuals. I quickly learned the importance of long-term care insurance for aging individuals and couples. If a person becomes very ill and/or disabled, they could potentially require home health care and assistance with daily activities or full-time care in a nursing home. The purpose of long-term care insurance is to pay for the costs of this type of medical care, which can be very expensive. A quality, well-run private nursing home currently costs around $5,000 to $6,000 per month. If a person is not independently wealthy, or what we refer to as self-insured, then these expenses can completely erode an individual's or a couple's retirement savings.

The solution from a financial planning perspective is to purchase long-term care insurance for your loved ones before they reach the age and stage of life when they need extensive medical care. Otherwise, the family will have to pay cash for the expenses related to home health care or a nursing home. Unexpected medical expenses are the number one risk factor for eroding a family's retirement savings. If you become completely indigent, meaning you have exhausted all of your financial resources, you could qualify for Medicaid. However, a nursing home paid for by Medicaid will be far from ideal care for you or your loved ones.

Many people mistakenly think that once they turn sixty-five, and are eligible for Medicare, that the insurance will also cover any long-term care needs in a nursing home if ever necessary. *This is false information.* Medicare *only* covers medically necessary acute care, such as doctor's visits, drugs, and hospital stays. Medicare coverage also focuses on short-term services for conditions that are expected to improve, such as physical therapy to help you regain your function after a fall or stroke.

I personally encouraged my parents to purchase long-term care insurance while they were still young and healthy so that the premiums for the insurance would be affordable. The two major factors for determining how expensive the premiums will be for a long-term care insurance policy are a person's age and current health status. *Please remember that insurance never gets cheaper if you wait a year to buy it in order to save money.* Unfortunately, you cannot help but get older every year, even if you're still in good health. Furthermore, an individual can be completely denied coverage if an insurance company believes they are too risky to insure. I personally have several clients who were denied coverage because they waited too long to apply for this type of insurance. Their health changed unexpectedly and they became too risky to insure for most long-term care insurance providers.

Taking Care of My Parents

In 2001, my parents went to a holiday party with friends. During the dinner party, my father gradually became extremely dizzy and nauseated. Fortunately, one of the guests at the party was in the medical field and knew immediately that my father was on the verge of having a heart attack. My father thought his friend was overreacting, but reluctantly allowed his friend to rush him to the nearest emergency room. His doctors immediately confirmed that he was in critical condition and he did in fact need immediate medical attention.

When my brother and I heard the news, we both drove as fast as possible to the hospital. I remember parking my car and running inside to find my parents in the Cardiac ICU. I was in such shock that I had no idea where I parked my car when I finally went to find it again. I'm telling you this story so you will know that I speak from experience that life can change in the blink of an eye. The point of the story is not to scare you. It's actually to teach you how to proactively plan for this type of situation from a financial planning perspective.

The physician said my father needed triple bypass heart surgery, and would definitely not be leaving the hospital any time soon. He ended up having heart bypass surgery on New Year's Eve. This was the first time in my life that I experienced the frightening reality that I might lose my father. Fortunately, my father's surgery was a success, and he eventually recovered from his heart surgery, but it was a very long journey. We were incredibly grateful he was still alive and with our family. However, his cardiologist told us that it was not a matter of if, but when, he would have another heart issue. That's difficult news to live with from a patient's point of view, as well as for the family members who love and depend on the person who has health challenges.

Before my father got sick, I encouraged him to purchase a joint long-term care insurance policy that would provide benefits for both of my parents if either one ever needed extensive medical care. I honestly hoped that they would never have to use the insurance. I knew from a risk mitigation standpoint that it was more prudent and cost effective to purchase a joint policy that both of my parents could benefit from financially, rather than an individual policy that would only provide benefits if one person became ill. I'd counseled many people already by that stage of my career. Well aware that no one knows what the future holds, I always tell my clients, "It's best to plan for the worst-case scenario, and hope for the best-case scenario."

Fortunately, with the help of modern medicine, my father's heart condition and blood pressure continue to be under control. He just celebrated his seventy-eighth birthday, and he's still working in his ministry part time, seventeen years after his heart surgery. He's not the type of retiree who plays golf or goes fishing a lot. Instead, he's passionate about using the time he has here on earth to further God's kingdom and bring more people to Christ. His ministry, Chapel of Hope, has started eight chapels in the Texas prison system. Today, these eight chapels alone host an estimated 80,000 inmate visits and 15,000 volunteer visits every year.

My mother has also been an active part of my father's ministry. However, about eight years ago we started noticing that her short-term memory was declining. She was still very active physically, but she was starting to show signs of confusion. After many visits to various doctors, specialists, and taking numerous tests, eventually she was diagnosed with dementia. Honestly, the news was quite devastating to her and our family. However, if you ask my mother, she would tell you that she's the most blessed woman on earth. She has two grown children who love and adore her, and eight healthy, active grandchildren. She's the picture of grace during a difficult trial. She loves God with all of her heart, mind, and soul.

After my father had triple bypass heart surgery, I always thought that he eventually would be the one to need part-time care, or full-time care in a nursing home. For the majority of the time my parents have had their long-term care insurance in place, it was never on my radar that my mom would be the one to benefit from the insurance.

After my mother received a formal diagnosis of dementia in 2013, she was able to begin collecting financial benefits from my parents' joint long-term care insurance. The financial benefits from her insurance have made a world of difference in terms of both of my parents' quality of life. One of the benefits of being medically qualified for financial benefits from your insurance is that you can stop paying the monthly or annual premiums. My father got a "raise" during retirement when he no longer had to cover the monthly insurance premiums with his fixed income.

The reality of life is that we don't know what the future holds. Thank God we can rest in the fact that God does have a plan for each and every one of us. I'm grateful that God has given me the tools to help not only my parents, but also people like you to mitigate the financial burdens that can arise unexpectedly in life. I can assure you that God does provide for each and every one of us, and he is faithful.

Purchasing Long-Term Care Insurance

If you or a loved one is in their fifties or sixties, it would be prudent to investigate the cost of purchasing long-term care insurance. The only reason not to at least investigate this type of insurance is if you are self-insured. In other words, you're fairly certain you have enough assets to pay for this type of medical care for as many years as you would need it. *Most people are not self-insured.* Remember, it does not cost anything to apply for coverage. You should contact a reputable insurance salesperson who is experienced with helping clients navigate the underwriting process for long-term care insurance.

There are many variables to consider when purchasing long-term care insurance:

- You must choose a waiting period before insurance benefits begin. The average waiting period is 90 to 180 days. The longer the waiting period, the cheaper the premiums for the insurance. However, if you don't have enough money to cover the medical care during the waiting period, then you need to select a shorter waiting period.
- You also need to select a monthly benefit amount. I usually recommend at least $5,000 per month, since the average cost of a nursing home runs around $5,000 to $6,000 per month.

- I advise my clients to select a cost of living adjustment (COLA) benefit so their insurance benefits keep up with inflation. The average COLA is three to five percent per year.
- When applying for coverage, you also need to select a time period for how long the benefits will last. Typically, you can choose to receive coverage for medical expenses in a nursing home for three to five years. However, if you end up utilizing home health care rather than care in a nursing home, your pool of money from your insurance will last longer.
- Make sure that you purchase coverage that offers flexibility for how you utilize your benefits if you, or your spouse, ever need them.

As you can see, purchasing long-term care insurance is *not* something you want to purchase online, or from an agent who is not experienced. Always seek wise counsel from a licensed insurance agent or financial advisor you know, or whom has been referred to you by a trusted resource. Also, take time to educate yourself on the different options you may want to add to a policy for yourself, your spouse, or your parents. If you're an educated consumer, you'll have more realistic options about the types of policies, options for coverage, premiums, and riders available in the marketplace today.

Of course other forms of insurance are absolutely necessary, such as medical, automobile, and home insurance. But as a personal financial advisor, I most often counsel my clients about life, disability, and long-term care insurance. I pray that this information has been helpful to you and may spare you some grief in times of trouble, should you or your family ever face such a time. Proper insurance to take care of your loved ones will give you peace of mind so you can move from fearful insecurity to confident control in regards to supporting your loved ones financially. Most important, please always remember the following: God himself is your best "refuge in the day of disaster" (Jer. 17:17).

How Much Life Insurance Do You Need to Protect Your Family?

	INCOME	
1.	Total annual income your family would need if you died today: What your family needs, before taxes, to maintain its current standard of living (typically between 60 to 75 percent of total income)	$
2.	Annual income your family would receive from other sources: Dividends, interest income, spouse's earnings, or Social Security	$
3.	Income to be replaced: *Subtract line 2 from line 1*	$
4.	Capital needed for income: *Multiply line 3 by appropriate factor in Table A*	$
	EXPENSES:	
5.	Funeral and other final expenses: The average cost of an adult funeral is about $6,130	$
6.	Mortgage and other outstanding debts: Include mortgage balance, credit card debt, car loans, etc.	$
7.	College costs for each child, in today's dollars: Average four-year costs: state college or university = $60,000 (in-state resident) Private college or out-of-state university = $100,000+	$
8.	Capital needed for college: Multiply line 7 by the appropriate factor in Table B	$
9.	Total capital required: *Add lines 4, 5, 6 and 8*	$
	ASSETS:	
10.	Savings and investments: Bank accounts, money market accounts, CDs, stocks, bonds, mutual funds, etc.	$
11.	Retirement savings: IRAs, 401(k)s, Keoghs, pension, and profit-sharing plans	$
12.	Present amount of life insurance: Include group insurance as well as insurance purchased on your own	$
13.	Total income-producing assets: *Add lines 10, 11, and 12*	$
14.	**Life insurance needed:** *Subtract line 13 from line 9*	**$**

TABLE A	
YEARS INCOME NEEDED	FACTOR
10	8.1
15	11.1
20	13.6
25	15.6
30	17.3
35	18.7
40	20.0

TABLE B	
YEARS UNTIL COLLEGE	FACTOR
5	.82
10	.68
15	.56
20	.46

Important note: Inflation is assumed to be four percent. The rate of return on investments is assumed to be eight percent. Changing either or both of these assumptions would change the results.

CHAPTER 7

Nobody Got Rich Paying Too Much for a House

> *Unless the LORD builds the house,*
> *the builders labor in vain.*
>
> Psalm 127:1

My husband and I have actually made money in real estate. It has taken sweat equity and vision for how each home could look after being renovated. I'm grateful to say the work over many years has paid off.

In 1998, my husband was in his early twenties. He decided early on that he wanted to invest in real estate. He was still a student on a very tight budget, but he was able to get a mortgage with affordable payments. He was very pleased because he was building equity and not just throwing away money on rent. After some careful research, he ended up choosing a condominium in a great location but in very bad shape cosmetically. He and his parents used sweat equity to paint, replace carpet, lay hardwood floors, and change out doors and hardware in order to give the home a facelift on a very small budget. He did all of this before I even met him.

After we married, I moved into the condo with my new husband. We quickly realized that a one-bedroom, loft-style condo was not very conducive to privacy. If one person worked or studied while the other person watched TV or slept, we had no sound barrier. So we sat down and analyzed our options. We met with a realtor that we trusted to find out how much we could realistically sell the condominium for. Then we researched the market to find out if we could afford a larger home, with at least two separate bedrooms.

We were excited to learn that my husband's sweat equity had paid off. He had made a very wise investment when he purchased his condominium in a very desirable location. However, if we really wanted to move into a larger home, we were going to have to buy a "fixer-upper" once again and use our sweat equity and profit from the sale of the condominium to do renovations and repairs. So that is exactly what we did, and we were fortunate that it all worked out. God was very gracious to us.

But then life happened, and we found out we were going to move to a different city for career reasons. We would have to sell our new little bungalow before we owned it for two years, which would mean any profits we made would be subject to capital gains taxes. Not good news. We spent months updating our home, and we knew that we could have potentially made a nice profit one day. But I did my research and sought wise counsel from an accountant. It turned out that there is an exception in the capital gains tax law if you have to move more than a certain number of miles for job relocation. So we were fortunate to be able to sell the bungalow for a very nice profit without paying any capital gains taxes.

When we moved to a new city, we then took the profit we made from the sale of the bungalow and bought a larger, slightly more expensive house in a very desirable location. This time we did not buy a fixer-upper. However, we bought a home that was vacant because the former owner was in the military and had been transferred overseas. A relocation company owned the house and they just wanted to sell it. For them, it was a nonemotional deal—the best type of seller. Most individuals who own a home are emotionally attached to it because their family has made special memories in the home. Homeowners often believe their house is worth more than it actually is, so emotional sellers can make the negotiation process much more difficult.

Since we knew the house we wanted to purchase was owned by a corporate entity, we made a very low offer, which was accepted. That particular home was one of the smallest houses in the neighborhood. We made sure the home was in an excellent school district for resale purposes. To make matters more interesting, there was a city zoning issue going on at the time we bought the house, related to some apartment complexes near that particular neighborhood. The home values were depressed a bit because people were nervous about the future property values. After a few years, the city and any potential buyers realized that the zoning issues were not a problem after all, and our entire neighborhood quickly escalated in value.

In the meantime, we became parents for the first time in 2006 to a sweet baby girl. One beautiful afternoon in 2007, I decided it was a great day to take the baby for a stroll around the neighborhood. Lots of our neighbors were outside when the weather was nice, and it was fun to stop and chat with people along the way. One of our neighbors had been unexpectedly widowed during the previous year, so I decided to check in on him to make sure he was doing all right. He told me that he was actually doing great. As a matter of fact, he was engaged to be married again.

He had been married for over fifty years, and his wife had only been gone about nine months. It was quite a shock. *What are the odds of that?* I thought to myself. So, I did what every good real estate investor would do in that situation, and I calmly asked him if he planned to move or stay in his house after he was remarried—very key information. He lived in a corner house on the largest lot in our neighborhood with tons of potential. We had driven past his house multiple times every day for years. We had always thought with some modifications, his home could be a great fit for our family. Never in our wildest imaginations did we think he would be moving out of his home anytime soon. Much to my surprise, he had already decided to sell his house once he figured out where he and his new wife would live after they were married.

So I went home and talked to my husband immediately. We knew all along that the house would need to be remodeled if we were to purchase it for our family. I told our neighbor not to do a thing to the house before he moved out, which he was thrilled about. This was a big blessing to him because he didn't have to go through the stress of putting his house on the market. We were able to purchase a home once again at a discounted price because it needed some work, and we did not use any real estate agents. He needed several months to get organized in order to actually move out. So he stayed in the house for about four more months. That allowed us the time we needed to finalize our renovation plans with our architect and contractors.

Once again, we made a wise investment in real estate, and you can do the same. But you have to be an educated, nonemotional buyer. Meanwhile, by word of mouth, we sold our existing home for a very nice profit, without paying any real estate commissions. A wonderful family purchased it, and they were not in a hurry to move in. They graciously allowed us to rent our house back from them, and stay in our existing home until we finished the construction on the new house. Thankfully, we only had to move once, and God worked out all of the details. This was the first time we ever thought we were buying our "forever home." We often joked that we would be buried in the backyard because we were never going to leave.

That was the plan, or so we thought.

My husband and I are adamant that we be good stewards of the resources that God has given us. Our home falls into this category. We have always wanted to make sure if we moved, that it was God's best plan for us. Moving does not scare us. However, doing something that is clearly out of God's will really frightens us.

In 2010, we became parents again for the second time, this time a boy. After a couple of years, we realized he wanted to be outside running and exploring freely. By 2013, the "forever home" we were living in was no longer conducive to our growing family's needs. We decided to do a little exploring. We found a house for sale on a good-size piece of property with a fishing pond, only ten minutes from the heart of the city and all of its conveniences—something extremely rare, especially for the price. The house needed a major overhaul, but we love interior design so that actually was a bonus to us. By that stage of our lives, we had a lot of practice. We could modify the house for our taste and our family's needs. Before we made any decisions, we asked God to confirm that this was in fact the right plan for us.

My husband had been saving money and planning for over a year to take his mother on a trip for her sixtieth birthday and his fortieth birthday. Even though he was going to be out of town, I decided to put some feelers out to see if anyone might be interested in our existing home. I put some pictures of our home on Facebook and gave some details about the house. I told my friends on Facebook to call me if they were interested in seeing the home in person.

My husband left on his trip on a Saturday morning, and I showed the house twice that same afternoon. We had a contract on the house the following day, and it was in escrow by Monday morning. God clearly confirmed that moving was in fact the right next step for us. So as soon as my husband got back in town, we started making plans for the new home in the country.

The funny thing is, I can't imagine living in a neighborhood now. I love the wide-open spaces and the beautiful scenery in the country. We are very blessed to have neighbors with children on either side of our property. I ring a large black dinner bell when it's time for the kids to come inside. The air is fresh, and my kids are learning how to climb trees and go fishing. Our neighbors not only consist of humans, but cows, ducks, donkeys, goats, and geese. It's a fun place to live and to grow up. We also truly love to have family and friends over to our home, in order to bless them with some entertainment and relaxation.

I now have an office attached to our home in the country where I can work and still keep an eye on our children. Interestingly, I have found that clients who come to my new home office often stay a little longer, and seem more at peace after our meetings than when they first arrived. My business has actually prospered more as a result of being in the country. Who would have ever thought? Only God.

Your Largest Investment: Your Home

I recently talked with a friend who did not think buying a house was an investment opportunity. She believes buying a home is more of a quality-of-life issue. In her opinion, you should simply purchase a home that is in a location, price range, and aesthetic that best fits your family's lifestyle. I respectfully listened to her theory and did not comment, but I could not disagree more. A house is a tangible real estate asset and definitely can be a good or bad investment. This really is not even a debate from a personal financial planning perspective. Buying a home may be one of the largest investments an individual, or a couple, will make in their lifetime.

Yes, you need to take into consideration your specific housing needs, such as the number of bedrooms your family may need, or finding a home in a good school district if you have children. You will definitely want to consider other lifestyle factors such as:

- How long will your commute to work be if you live in a certain location?
- Do you prefer a home in the suburbs, or do you want to live in the heart of the city?
- Do you want a two-story home, or do you need a one-story home because someone in your family has difficulty climbing stairs?
- Is a large yard a priority or not?

My professional opinion is that you can consider the practical housing needs of your family *and* make a wise investment with upside growth potential. For many people, the house they purchase will represent a large percentage of their assets and overall net worth. A house or condominium is tangible real estate and is a significant asset. Everything you own represents a portion of your overall net worth. What is your net worth? Here's a simple formula:

Net Worth = Total Assets - Total Liabilities

As I alluded to earlier, you can sell your primary residence after owning it for two years and pay no capital gains taxes on your profit up to $250,000. If you are married, you are exempt from capital gains taxes on profits up to $500,000. Please note that this tax law does not apply to second homes or investment properties. If you have a mortgage on your home, the interest and property taxes you pay while you own the home are both tax deductible. Your home can be one of your largest assets and also one of your most tax efficient investments.

Borrowing for a Home

It's very important to figure out a realistic budget before shopping for a home. This is not just a suggestion; it is sound, biblical advice. Jesus himself said, "Suppose one of you wants to build a tower. Won't you first sit down and estimate the cost to see if you have enough money to complete it?" (Luke 14:28).

Wouldn't it be fantastic if everyone could afford to pay cash outright for a new home? If you can do this, please do. However, this is not realistic for a large portion of the population. Many people cannot afford to pay for their homes outright with cash. If you cannot pay cash for a new house, you will want to get pre-qualified for a mortgage before you start house hunting. Remember, you will also need enough liquidity, or cash on hand, to make a down payment. Find out how much you will need for a down payment before you start shopping for a house. If you cannot make a down payment, then you are not ready to start looking for a new house to purchase. You will need more time to save money for your down payment.

I am often asked, "Is it still a good idea to purchase a home, rather than rent a home, even if you need a mortgage loan?"

My answer is, "Yes, if you plan to live there at least five years." If you make a wise choice when you purchase your home, and it's in a price range that you can easily afford, then you will build equity in a real estate asset. However, if you spend too much to renovate the home, sell the home before it appreciates in value, or live in the home for only a few years, you are unlikely to recoup your investment. Renovation costs, realtor fees, and other expenses will eat up the money you put into your home.

Many homeowners were stuck in their homes when the housing market crashed in 2008 because they had little to no equity in their homes when they were purchased. Prior to 2008, lenders were making it as easy as possible for people to purchase homes with down payments as little as *nothing*, but up to five percent. This was very common. They were also selling ARMS (Adjustable Rate Mortgage Loans) to naive borrowers, who didn't understand that their mortgage interest rate was only fixed for a certain period of years, and then it would escalate drastically.

Large banks and lenders were also not too concerned with making sure a borrower had a good credit history, or was actually able to afford the mortgage payments. They just wanted to sell as many mortgage loans as possible. All of a sudden, real estate values unexpectedly decreased and people were upside down in their homes. In other words, they owed more money than their house was worth. Some people were foreclosed upon, while others simply had to stay in their homes as long as they could afford the monthly mortgage payments. They had to wait until home values began to slowly appreciate again before they could even consider selling their homes. This was a wake-up call for many Americans.

Conventional mortgage loans are designed to be paid once per month for thirty years. I want to tell you about a couple of strategies for paying off your mortgage early. Instead of paying your mortgage payment once per month for 360 months, I suggest that you split your monthly mortgage payment in half, and pay every two weeks instead.

For example, my friends Dan and Catherine recently purchased a home with a mortgage balance of $300,000. Their interest rate is fixed for thirty years at four-and-a-half percent. If they pay their regular monthly mortgage, they will make twelve monthly payments of $1,520.06 = $18,240.72 (principal and interest) per year.

However, Dan and Catherine could pay their loan off almost five years earlier if they simply make biweekly mortgage payments, regardless of the day of the month on the calendar. There are 52 weeks in a year. Using this strategy, they will make twenty-six biweekly payments of $760.03 = $19,760.78. Using this strategy, an extra $1,520.06 will be paid each year to reduce the principal of the loan balance. As a result, the mortgage loan will be paid off 53 months faster and they will save $42,049.51 in interest expense. This strategy will allow them to pay their home off early and position them for retirement with no house payment.

Another strategy for paying off your home early is to choose a fifteen-year mortgage, rather than a twenty- or thirty-year mortgage. If you can afford the higher monthly payments, you will actually spend significantly less over the life of the loan. Traditionally, fifteen-year mortgage interest rates are lower than thirty-year mortgage interest rates. Please be sure to ask your banker about the pros and cons of a fifteen-year mortgage when purchasing a new home or refinancing your existing house or condominium.

I don't consider a mortgage loan a bad debt. Please understand that I'm not advising you to spend beyond your means. I am, however, advising you to make all of your money work as hard as possible, so that you can achieve financial freedom. If you're responsible with your mortgage loan payments, you will eventually own your home outright. If you continue to rent indefinitely, in order to avoid a mortgage loan, then you will never own a home.

As we discussed previously in chapter four, there is a big difference between what I consider bad debt and good debt. Bad debt encompasses credit card debt and other unsecured loans, which are loans that are obtained without the use of property as collateral for the loan. Bad debt also includes loans for cars, boats, or other types of vehicles that automatically depreciate in value the day you drive them off of the parking lot. Good debt is debt that is used wisely to purchase appreciating assets. If you make a wise purchase when you buy your home from an investment standpoint, your house will appreciate in value. Please remember that if you will have a mortgage on the home you wish to purchase, you must first make sure that you can comfortably afford the monthly payments. Otherwise, you should not be purchasing the home, even if it may appreciate in value one day.

Debt-to-income (DTI) ratio is a lending term that describes a person's monthly debt load in comparison to their monthly gross income. Mortgage loan officers use the debt-to-income ratio to determine whether an applicant can maintain payments on a given property. It helps both banks and prospective buyers to answer the question, "How much house can I afford?"

The debt-to-income ratio has nothing to do with the *willingness* of a person, or couple, to make their monthly mortgage payments. It simply measures a mortgage payment's economic burden on a household. Most mortgage guidelines enforce a maximum debt-to-income limit.

Most mortgage lenders require homeowners to have a debt-to-income ratio of forty percent or less. Shockingly, loan approvals are possible with DTIs of forty-five percent or higher. I don't recommend that your monthly housing budget get even close to forty percent of your monthly income. I think this is a very slippery slope.

My professional recommendation is that your entire monthly housing costs should not be more than twenty-five percent of your overall monthly budget. I believe that this is a much safer option financially. You want to make sure you always have adequate cash flow to cover all of your expenses. When figuring out how much house you can afford to buy, be sure to count *all* of your housing expenses, and not just the mortgage. You will have to pay property taxes every single year, and property taxes can be a significant annual expense, depending upon the tax laws for the state and city in which you live. I also advise my clients to find out what the average cost of utilities will be for the home each month, and whether or not the home is located in a neighborhood or building that requires you to pay homeowner's dues and/or maintenance fees.

Please don't forget to include the expense of maintaining, decorating, and furnishing your home in your monthly budget. If the home is older or in poor condition, it's likely to incur more maintenance costs than a newer, well-maintained home, but may be less expensive to purchase initially. Still, repair and maintenance costs can mount quickly. So when you buy a home, please keep an eye on what you may need to spend on maintenance in the following categories:

- Lawn, tree care, and pool maintenance if applicable
- Roof maintenance
- Furnace and/or air conditioner
- Plumbing
- Electrical
- Basement renovations or improvements
- Appliances
- Flooring such as carpet, tile, or hardwood
- Siding, rock, or brick work
- Indoor and outdoor paint
- Driveway and sidewalks
- Doors and windows
- Deck and/or fencing
- Furniture and interior decorations

Purchasing a Home

Once you have established a realistic housing budget, then you can start the fun part, which is house hunting. The number-one rule during the house hunting adventure is to not look at homes that are over your budget. Be careful if you're working with a realtor who is not listening to your specific requests. Many realtors are very persuasive and often try to push their clients up into a higher price point. The more money you spend on a home, the higher the realtor's commission will be, so it's not rocket science to figure out that they can have a conflict of interest. Definitely not all realtors, but some realtors, will show a prospective buyer a beautiful, sparkly, shiny house in a price range that they simply cannot easily afford. This is dangerous from a financial planning standpoint. Before you know it, you'll be trying to rationalize ways to afford a more expensive home.

I'm speaking from experience when I tell you that you can still enjoy living in your home, while making a wise investment. It does take discipline though. As I have shared before, my husband and I have purchased several homes in very desirable locations that needed some work to bring the house back to life. We were able to "buy low and sell high" after we renovated the homes. If you purchase a home that is brand new from a home builder, or that has already been recently renovated, you're most likely going to pay top dollar. The seller is going to place the price of the home at the higher end of the market because they want to recoup their building or renovation costs. Keep these facts in mind when you consider purchasing a new home:

- Make sure you have enough money for a down payment before you begin looking.
- Have a realistic monthly budget that allows you to tithe, save, and then spend the rest.
- Make sure your overall monthly housing expenses do not account for more than twenty-five percent of your total monthly budget.
- Do not allow a realtor to show you houses that you cannot afford. It's just too easy to fall in love and then be tempted to justify buying a home at a price that exceeds your budget.
- *Your first home will most likely not be your forever home.* Do your homework and make intelligent investments in real estate so you can make a profit when you sell your home in the future.

As long as you're an educated, nonemotional buyer with realistic expectations about how much house you can actually afford, definitely consider investing in real estate. A house may be one of the largest purchases you ever make. It can serve several different purposes. Obviously, it will provide shelter for you and your family, which is one of our primary needs as humans. However, it's also a place where precious family memories can be made that will be cherished for many years. A home should be a peaceful place to rest and recharge your batteries. It can also be a wise investment financially.

We've mainly been talking about purchasing a home for the first time. However, seniors and retirees face some different circumstances that can affect their housing decisions. If a senior needs to get equity out of a home for the following reasons, then it may make sense to sell and purchase a less expensive home, or become a renter again:

- Need more income to support themselves during retirement
- Need to downsize due to challenges with maintenance
- Need to move to a nursing home or assisted living facility

Every couple or individual's situation is unique. An important point to remember when you're no longer working during retirement is that your fixed income needs to adequately cover all of your home's expenses, not just the mortgage.

If you're retired and debt free with no mortgage, congratulations! However, you do still need to consider whether your monthly maintenance, utilities, property taxes, and/or possible homeowner's fees are affordable when deciding where to live during retirement. For some people, it may make the most financial sense to become a renter, as opposed to a homeowner. Renting may allow more financial freedom by eliminating any unexpected expenses related to maintenance and home repairs, as well as annual property taxes. You cannot afford to be living month-to-month, trust me! Retirement is the time in your life to be on autopilot with your budget and monthly housing costs.

Retirement is certainly a season in life when it makes sense to seek wise counsel from a financial advisor or trusted person. They can help you determine which housing plan makes the most sense for you and your unique circumstances. One size does not fit all.

Whether you're buying your first home or your tenth home, please be sure to do your homework before you start house hunting. Be careful not to get emotionally attached to a home in a price range that you simply cannot afford. Pray for guidance before you make any final decisions about the house you will purchase. I do believe that if you ask God for wisdom, he will guide you to your new home. "Trust in the LORD with all your heart and lean not on your own understanding; in all your ways submit to him, and he will make your paths straight" (Prov. 3:5–6). Wise investments in real estate can help move you from fearful insecurity to confident control of your personal finances.

CHAPTER 8

When Can I Transition from Making Money to Spending It?

SECRET #8: THE FAITHFUL INVEST FOR RETIREMENT

Invest in seven ventures, yes, in eight;
you do not know what disaster may
come upon the land.

Ecclesiastes 11:2

My friend Shay is a woman who is quite busy, both personally and professionally. She's a teacher, a single mother, and the owner of a personal fitness business. Shay recently told me that in her community of mostly African-Americans, people are taught to work hard and earn an income, but are not taught to take risks with their personal finances. As a result, Shay sees many people who aren't building wealth. In order to build wealth, you will have to take some risk through investing or starting a business of your own. It does take hard work.

Shay believes that by helping others achieve their goals through fitness, she is also helping them emotionally, physically, and spiritually. Shay enhances and improves the quality of other people's lives. She earns more money counseling and training other people to live healthier lifestyles than she earns as a teacher. As she helps others achieve their fitness goals, she is simultaneously growing her assets and overall wealth. While we will spend most of this chapter looking at financial investments, don't forget that your most important investment will always be the investment of your time and your talents.

Friend, please know that growing wealth and being wise with our most precious assets—our time, talent, and resources—is biblical. God blesses those who work hard and make wise decisions. Here is what Jesus had to say about investing wisely. The story is a familiar one, but it's worth rereading in full because it vividly dramatizes what God expects us to do with what he's given us.

The Parable of the Bags of Gold

"Again, it will be like a man going on a journey, who called his servants and entrusted his wealth to them. To one he gave five bags of gold, to another two bags, and to another one bag, each according to his ability. Then he went on his journey. The man who had received five bags of gold went at once and put his money to work and gained five bags more. So also, the one with two bags of gold gained two more. But the man who had received one bag went off, dug a hole in the ground and hid his master's money.

"After a long time the master of those servants returned and settled accounts with them. The man who had received five bags of gold brought the other five. 'Master,' he said, 'you entrusted me with five bags of gold. See, I have gained five more.'

"His master replied, 'Well done, good and faithful servant! You have been faithful with a few things; I will put you in charge of many things. Come and share your master's happiness!'

"The man with two bags of gold also came. 'Master,' he said, 'you entrusted me with two bags of gold; see, I have gained two more.'

"His master replied, 'Well done, good and faithful servant! You have been faithful with a few things; I will put you in charge of many things. Come and share your master's happiness!'

"Then the man who had received one bag of gold came. 'Master,' he said, 'I knew that you are a hard man, harvesting where you have not sown and gathering where you have not scattered seed. So I was afraid and went out and hid your gold in the ground. See, here is what belongs to you.'

"His master replied, 'You wicked, lazy servant! So you knew that I harvest where I have not sown and gather where I have not scattered seed? Well then, you should have put my money on deposit with the bankers, so that when I returned I would have received it back with interest.

"'So take the bag of gold from him and give it to the one who has ten bags. For whoever has, will be given more, and they will have an abundance. Whoever does not have, even what they have will be taken from them.'"

Matthew 25:14–29

What do you think this parable is trying to teach us? Quite simply, God wants you to be a wise steward of the money and assets he has given you. What is a wise steward? Let's start with a quick glance at Webster's dictionary: "Steward: A noun, a person employed to manage another's property, esp. a large house or estate; a person whose responsibility it is to take care of something."

So how do we become the kind of person who manages well what God has entrusted to us? Let's make this as simple as possible. Just remember: 10/10/10/70.

- **10**: The first ten percent of your income should be a tithe and offering to God (see chapter three).
- **10**: The second ten percent of your income should be put in a very safe investment or money market account for future liquidity needs (see chapter five).
- **10**: The third ten percent of your income should be invested wisely to outpace inflation and grow over time.
- **70**: The remaining seventy percent of your income should be spent wisely on items you need and/or want.

In this chapter, we'll learn about the third ten percent of your monthly income. I want you to consider investing it wisely in order to grow and appreciate over time. Benjamin Franklin is famous for saying, "A penny saved is a penny earned." This is not necessarily true. If you invest wisely, you can actually *multiply* your money, not just add it. In other words, with wise and strategic investing, a penny saved may turn into five pennies.

Growing Your Assets with Compound Interest

There are many different instruments, or products, available today to help grow your assets with interest. If you invest in the following types of investments, you can benefit from compound interest:

- Money market cash accounts
- Bank certificates of deposit (often referred to as CDs)
- Bonds
- Annuities

Compound interest is interest added to the principal of a deposit, or loan, so that the added interest also earns interest from then on. This addition of interest to the principal is called *compounding*. A bank account may have its interest compounded every year. For example, an account with $1,000.00 of initial principal and five percent interest per year would have a balance of $1,050.00 at the end of the first year, $1,102.50 at the end of the second year, $1,157.62 at the end of the third year, and so on. Remember, the harder your money works, the less *you* have to work.

There is a well-known calculation you can perform to determine how many years it will take to double your money. It's called *The Rule of 72*. You divide seventy-two by the annual interest rate you are receiving on your investment and it will tell you how long it will take to double your money. For example, if I invest $100,000 in a money market account earning one percent per year, it will take me seventy-two years ($72/1 = 72$) to double my money. On the other hand, if I invest $100,000 in a mutual fund earning eight percent per year, it will take me only nine years to double my investment and have $200,000 ($72/8 = 9$).

It takes time for money to grow. In a world bent on quick money, we must remember this principle. Many people have lost their entire savings because they trusted in a get-rich-quick scheme. Be very cautious if a broker promises an extremely high rate of return that is obviously unrealistic.

Growing Your Assets by Capital Appreciation

Besides compound interest, you can also grow your investments by capital appreciation. The following investments increase in value as the underlying investment, or capital, appreciates in value:

- Stocks
- Mutual funds containing stock
- Business assets
- Variable annuities

- Tangible real estate such as a home or office building
- REITs (real estate investment trusts), which are portfolios of commercial real estate that investors can purchase shares of, similar to a mutual fund
- Commodities
- Some coins and fine jewelry

Investors versus Speculators

If you truly are an investor, you're definitely not putting money in the lottery or gambling. Investors take a long-term approach to growing their wealth. They plant the seed, then water the seed, and then watch the tree grow over time. It's a process. This is called investing, not speculation.

A speculator, as opposed to an investor, does not take into account the overall risk of a portfolio. Speculators try to "hit it big" by investing in one new idea or product. Tech companies offering brand-new technology are examples of speculative investments. The company doesn't have a track record, but the product is supposed to be the next big thing. Speculators take large risks in the hope of making quick money. I never advise anyone to make speculative investments unless the money invested truly is fun money. In other words, if you lost every single penny you made in a speculative investment, you and your family would not suffer financially.

An important question to consider is, "Am I an investor or a speculator?" Investors save and invest systematically every month. They focus on buying good solid investments that are allocated to a well-diversified portfolio. They do not get emotional about daily movements in the stock market indices. Their investment approach is often referred to as a "buy and hold" strategy. Another very important quality of a good investor is to have assets that are non-correlated to one another. Non-correlated assets do not increase or decrease at the same time. For example, stocks and bonds do not usually both increase or decrease at the same time. The overall goal with investing is to grow your assets, while also managing your investment risk. A good investment strategy will minimize volatility (the ups and downs of the market) and maximize your security.

One way to take volatility out of your investment portfolio is the use of dollar-cost averaging. Dollar-cost averaging is a technique of buying a fixed dollar amount of a particular investment on a regular schedule, regardless of the share price. More shares are purchased when prices are low, and fewer shares are bought when prices are high. Eventually, the average cost per share of the security will become smaller and smaller. Dollar-cost averaging lessens the risk of investing a large amount in a single investment at the wrong time.

No one has a crystal ball. If you ever have an advisor guarantee you anything, please be very skeptical. This is why it's so important to balance your risk when you invest money. You certainly don't want to keep your money under a mattress to avoid any volatility, but you also want to be prudent about your investments.

Investment Risk

The word *risk* has a negative sound to it. However, if we break risk down into the components of what it stands for in terms of investing, it begins to be a little more manageable. I promise that you will be better equipped to manage your money effectively if you understand the different types of risk. Long-term investing, or the buy-and-hold strategy, as well as diversification, are some of the most effective strategies you can use to help manage investment risk. But, unfortunately, there are no fail-proof guarantees against investment loss. Let me explain the different types of investment risk.

Inflation Risk

Risk from inflation is the danger that inflation will reduce your purchasing power and the returns from your investments. If your savings and investments are failing to outpace inflation, you might consider investing in growth-oriented alternatives such as stocks, stock mutual funds, variable annuities, or other vehicles. The current inflation rate hovers around two percent, which means your investments will need to make over two percent in order for you to gain any money from your investment.

Interest Rate Risk

A bond is simply an IOU in which an investor agrees to loan money to a company or government, in exchange for a predetermined interest rate for a predetermined length of time. Bonds and other fixed-income investments tend to be sensitive to changes in interest rates. When interest rates rise, the value of these investments falls. After all, why would someone pay full price for your bond at three percent when new bonds are being issued at five percent? The opposite is also true. When interest rates fall, existing bonds increase in value.

Economic Risk

When the economy experiences a downturn, the earnings capabilities of most firms are threatened. While some industries and companies adjust to downturns in the economy very well, others such as large industrial firms take longer to react. Their capital outlays may be more than their revenue and can take a while to turn positive again.

Market Risk

A "security" is a catchall term for many kinds of investments. When a market experiences a downturn, it tends to pull down the value of most of its securities with it. Afterward, the affected securities will recover at rates more closely related to the fundamental strength of the corporation and specific business. Market risk affects almost all types of investments, including stocks, bonds, real estate, and others. Historically, long-term investing has been a way to minimize the effects of market risk, since markets generally rise over a long period of time.

Specific Risk

Events may occur that only affect a specific company or industry. For example, the death of a young company's president may cause the value of the company's stock to drop. It's almost impossible to pinpoint all of the specific risks of a company, but diversifying your investments could help manage the effects of such risks.

I can speak from experience that managing risk is crucial to weathering the ups and downs of the stock market. Not only do I manage my family's money, but I'm also responsible for my clients' investment accounts that I manage as their financial advisor. I know intellectually that I must invest in stocks, or equities, to allow my investments to grow more than inflation over the long term. As a result, there will also be some volatility over time.

You may be surprised to hear this, but the ups and downs in my clients' accounts affect me more emotionally than the volatility in my own investment accounts. That is why I always make sure that the portfolios I manage are extremely well diversified. I do not speculate on anything. I feel an extreme responsibility to protect and grow my clients' wealth. I consider it an honor and a compliment that someone has entrusted me with their money. If I do not practice what I preach by utilizing both diversification and asset allocation tools when selecting investments, I wouldn't be able to sleep at night. I would be on a constant roller coaster of emotion as the Dow Jones Industrial Average or the S&P 500 Index increased or decreased each day.

Qualified versus Non-Qualified Investment Accounts

I'm often asked about the difference between non-qualified assets and qualified assets. These are confusing terms to people not working in the financial services industry. Non-qualified assets consist of accounts that are readily accessible and *not* invested in retirement accounts. They are also called taxable assets. Examples of non-qualified assets consist of the following types of accounts:

- Checking account: a simple depository account held at a bank or a credit union used for immediate liquidity needs and check-writing privileges.
- Savings account: a depository account used to set aside funds in order to earn interest. These accounts are also held at a bank or credit union.
- Brokerage accounts: investment accounts not earmarked for retirement, that can hold a variety of investment vehicles such as stocks, bonds, cash, etc.
- Non-qualified annuities: retirement savings vehicles that are funded with after-tax dollars. Non-qualified annuities are not included inside a retirement account wrapper, such as an IRA.

In contrast, a qualified account is simply a retirement account. The following qualified accounts are primarily used to save for retirement:

- Roth IRA account: funds are deposited after-tax in a Roth IRA account and grow tax-free for life. The owner of the account has discretion over how the funds are invested. There is no penalty for withdrawal of funds as long as the funds are withdrawn after age 59½. Exceptions to this rule include withdrawals after five years for a first-time home purchase, or education costs for dependents.
- Traditional IRA: funds are deposited pre-tax in a traditional

IRA and will grow tax-deferred for life, until withdrawn. Withdrawals are taxed as ordinary income. Hopefully, a retiree will be in a much lower tax bracket when funds are withdrawn. Similar to a Roth IRA, there is no penalty for withdrawals as long as funds are withdrawn after age 59½.

- 401(k) plan: a company sponsored retirement plan that allows employers and employees to contribute funds to a tax-deferred account for the benefit of the employee. Taxation is similar to that of a traditional IRA and withdrawals are also free of penalties after age 59½.

- 403(b) plan: this type of retirement plan works exactly the same way as a corporate 401(k) plan. However, 403(b) plans are only offered by employers in the nonprofit arena. Examples include: school districts, government agencies, hospitals, and not-for-profit organizations.

Measuring Market Performance through Indices

You may be asking yourself right about now, "What really is the Dow Jones Industrial Average, or DOW, as it is frequently referred to? What is the S&P 500 Index? What index do they use to measure the performance of bonds?" All of these are benchmark indices used to measure the value of a section of the market.

The Dow Jones Industrial Average (DJIA) is a price-weighted average of only thirty significant stocks traded on the New York Stock Exchange and the Nasdaq Index. Charles Dow originally invented the DJIA back in 1896. Often referred to as "the Dow," the DJIA is one of the oldest and single most-watched indices in the world. The DJIA includes companies like General Electric, Disney, Exxon, and Microsoft. When the TV networks say, "The market is up today," they are generally referring to the Dow Jones Industrial Average.

The S&P 500 Index contains five hundred stocks chosen for market size, liquidity, and industry grouping, among other factors.

The S&P 500 is designed to be a leading indicator of US stocks. The purpose of the index is to reflect the risk/return characteristics of the large cap universe of stocks. Companies included in this index are selected by Index Committee members of the S&P 500, a team of analysts and economists at Standard & Poor's. The S&P 500 is a market-value-weighted index. Each stock's weight is proportionate to its market value.

The S&P 500 is one of the most commonly used benchmarks for the overall US stock market. The Dow Jones Industrial Average (DJIA) was at one time the most renowned index for US stocks, but because the DJIA contains only thirty companies, most people agree that the S&P 500 is a better representation of the US market. In fact, many consider it to be the definition of the market.

The Lehman Aggregate Bond Index is an index used by bond funds as a benchmark to measure relative performance of different types of securities. The index includes government securities, mortgage-backed securities, asset-backed securities, and corporate securities. The maturities of the bonds in the index are more than one year.

If you are invested in a diversified portfolio, and *not* an index mutual fund that tracks any of these indices, then you do not need to worry about the performance of these indices on a daily basis. I never invest my money, or any of my client's money, solely in an index fund. I would consider that passive investing.

Instead, I utilize active money managers that have portfolios that are appropriate for each client's individual needs, risk tolerance, time horizon, and goals. One size certainly does not fit all clients. As a result, the investment accounts my firm manages will not mimic these indices. They will not go up as much, or down as much, as these indices fluctuate and change. This is an important concept to remember, especially if you listen to news channels on a frequent basis that sensationalize changes in the stock market indices.

Another myth is that small investors can only start investing money if they purchase an index fund. That's simply not true. There is a universe of available mutual funds that are well diversified and actively managed. Some only require a minimum investment of fifty dollars per month.

You may have also heard people say that investing is really easy. "Just buy yourself a good index mutual fund and let your money ride. Don't worry about it." You hear this when the stock market is performing well, which is called a bull market. The opposite of a bull market is a bear market, which means stocks are continually losing value. *I've found through years of experience that everyone is a stockbroker in bull markets.*

Some investors think I have failed if the assets in their portfolio temporarily decrease in value. They call me in a panic and they want to bail out of the market. This is the worst mistake I see investors make. They get extremely worried as soon as their investment portfolio experiences any volatility. What they do not understand is that the process is a marathon and not a sprint.

A money manager really earns their stripes when the stock market is going down and not up. It's pretty easy to make money when the stock market is flying high in a bull market. In a bull market share prices of stocks are rising and expected to continue to rise as well. I often joke, "During bull markets, I feel like I can throw things on a dart board and make money, and everyone thinks I'm a hero." I'm not a hero. I'm just doing my job.

As money managers, we are graded based on benchmarks. We normally use the S&P 500 Index as a benchmark for a stock, or equity, portfolio. We also use the Lehman Aggregate Bond Index as a benchmark for a bond portfolio. These benchmarks help us to measure our performance, but your individual investment results may vary from the benchmarks.

For example, a client might have sixty percent of her assets in the stock market while forty percent is invested in the bond market or fixed income and cash. I do this to diversify the client's portfolio, making sure all her eggs are not in one basket (more on that below). If my client's portfolio increases in value by eight percent while the S&P 500 Index rises by fourteen percent, she might be angry and think I'm doing a poor job of managing her money. I often have to reiterate to new investors that they are not 100 percent invested in the stock market. That would be foolish. If I'm doing my job, my client's investment accounts will never increase in value as much as the stock market index increases on any single day, and it will *never* decrease in value as much as the stock market tumbles on any one bad day. A portion of their money is invested in the stock market, and a portion is invested in more conservative, or fixed income, investments. This is done purposefully and strategically to give investors upside potential with downside protection.

The Importance of Asset Allocation

Together, before I ever invest any money, my clients and I both agree upon the best asset mix for their individual account. In other words, we determine what percentage of their overall portfolio should be invested in stocks, bonds, real estate, cash, and so on. This strategy is called asset allocation. We make this decision based on the following criteria:

- How much of their overall net worth are we investing?
- The client's age
- The client's risk tolerance
- Time frame for investing
- Tax considerations

The key to successful investing is managing risk while maintaining the potential for adequate returns on your investments. One of the most effective ways to help manage your investment risk is to diversify the assets in your overall portfolio. The purpose of diversification is to manage risk by spreading your money across a variety of investments such as stocks, bonds, real estate, commodities, and cash alternatives. However, please remember that diversification does not guarantee a profit or protect against loss.

The main philosophy behind diversification is quite simple: "Don't put all of your eggs in one basket." As investment managers, we spread out risk in our clients' portfolios among different investment categories, as well as over several different industries and even geographic regions. Diversification can help offset a loss in any one investment.

The power of diversification will most likely help smooth out your total investment returns over time. As one investment increases, it may offset the decreases in another. This will allow your portfolio to ride out market fluctuations, providing a more steady performance under various economic conditions. By potentially reducing the impact of market ups and downs, diversification could go far in enhancing your comfort level with investing.

Diversification is one of the main reasons that mutual funds may be attractive to both experienced and novice investors. Many noninstitutional investors have a limited investment budget and may find it challenging to construct a portfolio that is sufficiently diversified. For a modest initial investment, you can purchase shares in a diversified portfolio of securities called a mutual fund. These funds offer investors built-in diversification. Depending on the objectives of the mutual fund, it may contain a variety of stocks, bonds, and cash vehicles, or a combination of them.

It's quite interesting to me that diversification is part of what's called modern portfolio theory. However, it's discussed in the Bible that was written thousands of years ago: "Invest in seven ventures, yes, in eight; you do not know what disaster may come upon the land" (Eccl. 11:2). This is the definition of diversification of assets. We can make wise assessments of market conditions, but nobody knows for certain what the future holds. If a financial advisor or money manager ever guarantees you anything, please be skeptical. You really need to spread your assets out among a variety of asset classes. Then you will not be overexposed to any particular investment or asset class. Please remember, money managers do not have a crystal ball. No one does.

Whether you're investing in mutual funds, self-directing your own combination of stocks, bonds, and other investment vehicles, or working with a money manager, it is wise to understand the importance of asset allocation and diversifying the assets inside of your accounts. The value of individual stocks, bonds, and mutual funds will fluctuate over time depending upon market conditions. Just make sure you're not overly exposed to any one single stock or investment. I want to remind you again that you are not in control. Investing is simply the management of odds.

Socially Responsible Investing (SRI), or Social Investment

Because I'm overtly Christian, I often get asked about my opinion on socially responsible investing (SRI). Socially conscious investors view a corporation's practices as it relates to environmental stewardship and human rights, not just profitability, when deciding how to invest their money. They may also choose to avoid investments in businesses involved in products that they do not support. Examples of industries often avoided by socially responsible investors include: alcohol, tobacco, gambling, and pornography.

I personally think SRI is a great idea as long as it's used for good to bring about positive social changes in society. However, it should never be used as a way to alienate any segment of the population unjustly, such as a specific ethnicity or nationality.

Investments that Generate Passive Income

When you invest money in order to generate interest income, capital appreciation, or hopefully both, you are seeking what is known as passive income. Passive income is very important in the pursuit of financial freedom. Passive income is also known as "unearned income." It's an income stream that you receive on a regular basis, with little effort required to maintain it. This is a key component to building wealth. Someone, or something, has to generate income to support you and your family. Wouldn't you rather your money work harder so you don't have to? Another term for passive income that I like is "mailbox money." Some people think that passive income is about getting something for nothing. Passive income is not a get-rich-quick scheme. There is still work involved initially to create the income stream. Some people will use passive income to supplement their salary, while others will take advantage of passive income to fund their retirement years. Here are some common strategies for generating passive income.

Dividend-Yielding Stocks

Dividend-yielding stocks are purchased in order to provide the investor with an income stream. "Dividend yield" is a calculation used to determine how much income the investor will receive for each dollar invested. Owning dividend-yielding stocks is definitely one of the most common ways to generate a passive income stream.

Many novices to the stock market jump in without investigating the financial statements of the company that is issuing the stock. This can be risky. Please watch out for "dividend traps." If a corporation offers a dividend yield, or income stream, equal to ten percent or more annually, it's probably a pretty risky investment.

Rental Properties

This is an effective and time-honored way of earning passive income. However, it requires more work and investment expertise than people might expect. You have to do your due diligence on the real estate properties you consider purchasing in order to make a wise investment. If you want to earn passive income from a rental property, you must analyze the following investment factors:

- The purchase price of the property
- The costs and expenses of properly maintaining the property
- Whether there is a rental market for the home
- The return on investment
- The financial risks of owning the property

Prices for rental homes can vary dramatically depending upon the city and state in which you live. For example, a home in a small to medium-size town in the Midwest states will be much less expensive than a home or condominium in Los Angeles, New York City, Dallas, or Chicago. You really need to do your homework *before* you try investing in real estate to create a passive income.

Let me give you an example of how this works in real life. Let's say your personal goal is to earn $24,000 a year in rental income. You have a mortgage on a property that requires a $1,500 monthly payment. Your rental property also requires an additional $300 per month in taxes and other expenses to maintain the property. In order to reach your goal of $24,000 of passive income per year (average of $2,000 per month), you will need to charge at least $3,800 in rent each month. Now the question becomes one of risk: Is there a market for your property? Is $3,800 per month a reasonable price to charge for monthly rent in the specific area where the home is located? What if you get an irresponsible tenant? Will your tenant damage the property? All of these factors could result in a sizable deduction in your passive income *and* your underlying investment in real estate. Once again, my best advice is to do lots of research before you take the plunge into investing in rental properties to create passive income.

Royalties

Some people fantasize about creating passive income by writing a book or selling some product. They picture themselves sitting back while cash from the sales of these products just rolls in. This is often touted among internet marketing gurus as an easy, sure-fire way to create a passive income stream. While these products can eventually yield an excellent income stream, creating them is hardly a passive activity. It takes a large amount of time, energy, and creativity to create, market, and sell the product. Most importantly, the product has to be something that people are willing to pay money for.

Affiliate Marketing

Website owners or bloggers promote a third party's product by including a link to the product on their site. If a visitor clicks on the link and makes a purchase from the third party, the site owner receives a commission, generally around fifteen to twenty percent. Income generated by affiliate marketing is considered passive because, in theory, you can earn money just by adding the link to your website. In reality, you have to find a way to attract readers to your site, so that they click on the link, and buy something. It is an ongoing marketing project. A good example of this is Ruth Soukup, who created the *Living Well Spending Less* blog. A large portion of her income comes from affiliate marketing, as well as marketing her own products on how to be a successful blogger.

Peer-to-Peer (P2P) Lending

Peer-to-peer lending is a new way of creating passive income. A person, rather than a bank, acts as a lender in order to earn returns as high as eight to twelve percent. A P2P loan is a personal loan facilitated through a third-party intermediary, such as www.Prosper.com or www.LendingClub.com. At $3.5 trillion, the consumer credit market is a significant and often overlooked component of the bond market. It yields more than all major fixed income sectors by at least 2x.[1]

The loans are unsecured so a lender must be aware of the risk of default. It is wise to diversify a lending portfolio by investing smaller amounts over multiple loans. The time it takes to master the metrics is just one of the reasons that P2P lending isn't entirely passive. Since you're investing in multiple loans, you really need to pay close attention to payments received and other bookkeeping requirements. I only recommend P2P lending for savvy investors.

Converting Investments to Income

Eventually the day will come: your last day of work. You will need to transition from working full time to retirement and enjoying other pursuits. And instead of working and saving your money, you will start using your investments (instead of your salary) to support your lifestyle.

One of my favorite illustrations of a successful transition from working full time to enjoying her retirement years is my client Bonnie Goldman. She and her husband Seth were both educators, working hard for over thirty years both as teachers and school administrators. They were quite frugal and always made sure to fully participate in their teacher retirement plans. They were never wealthy by the world's standards, but they lived a comfortable middle-class lifestyle throughout their adult lives on the East Coast. They were the proud parents of twin boys that they made sure were well educated and successfully launched into careers of their own.

Unfortunately, Seth died unexpectedly in 2007, just before he and Bonnie were officially going to retire from the school districts where they had worked for so many years. Seth never got to enjoy his retirement with Bonnie. However, he did give her the gift of being financially prepared for his passing. He left a legacy of loving God, working hard, and making wise financial decisions for his wife and his sons. Seth had a generous life insurance policy that provided for his wife and their twin boys, as well as a will and an estate plan that were both very well thought out. He was also extremely organized, which is an amazing gift to leave for the beneficiaries of your estate.

His careful financial planning allowed Bonnie time to grieve before making any long-term decisions about how she would live in retirement as a single widow, rather than with her husband as she had always envisioned. This was a shattered dream for Bonnie. However, after taking time to grieve, pray, and consult her friends and family, she decided to move to Texas to spend her retirement years close to one of her sons and her beloved grandchildren.

This is when I met Bonnie for the first time. We immediately had a lot in common. She is very wise, but also quite funny, even though I don't think she intends to be. Every time I gave her investment advice she would proclaim, "From your mouth to God's ears." My husband and I use that phrase often now in our own lives.

One of the first things we did from a financial planning perspective was to create a realistic monthly budget for Bonnie. Together, we reviewed her monthly recurring expenses and then decided how much she could afford to spend each month in retirement. She had a pension from the school district, but she needed to supplement her monthly income. We used a portion of her assets to buy an annuity. An annuity would provide her with additional income each month. We purchased her annuity inside an IRA so she is only taxed as she takes income out of the annuity over time, and not all at once. The annuity provided her with the following benefits:

- A guaranteed income stream for life that she could never outlive
- Access to cash inside of the annuity if she ever has a liquidity need
- A death benefit for her two sons

It was very important to Bonnie to leave assets to her sons and grandsons as part of her legacy. Therefore, we decided to use some of her taxable assets to pay for a term life insurance policy with a lump sum of cash to replace some of her investments she would use to live on. We also used a portion of her taxable trust funds to pay off the small mortgage she had on her new home in Texas. That allowed Bonnie to live debt free as well as rent free. The remaining trust funds were invested in a conservative investment portfolio that she could access if needed. She uses some of these funds each year to travel the world with her dear friends from the synagogue.

As we fast forward to 2017, Bonnie is the poster child for a successful transition into retirement, even though her journey has not been easy. I have seen her blossom and become a very strong, independent, and inspiring woman. She is very involved in the lives of her grandchildren, and she hosts all of the Jewish holidays at her home with her family. She is also a docent at our local modern art museum. The museum has inspired her so much artistically that she now also takes classes to learn how to paint with watercolors. She travels all over the world, literally, as she says, "While I still can." She is busier in retirement than she was when she was working full time.

Purchasing an Annuity

Most people spend a large portion of their adult life accumulating assets. We work so we can have money to cover our family's needs. If we are wise, we save a portion of our income every month. How do we know when we can finally stop working and start living off of the income that our assets will provide?

This transition period is called "moving from the accumulation phase of assets to the annuitization of assets." It may sound like fancy, financial jargon, but it is a very important aspect of financial planning. Accumulation of assets simply means working and saving money. Annuitization of assets means taking the money you already have, and figuring out how to create an income stream for yourself.

The decline of traditional pensions, combined with longer life spans and rising medical expenses, has created an uncertain future for many Americans, including those who have put away a solid nest egg for retirement. Many people are fearful that they are going to outlive their retirement savings. This is one of the reasons you should consider purchasing an annuity.

An annuity is a contract between you and your insurance company, in which you make a lump sum payment or series of payments, and in return, you receive regular disbursements beginning either immediately or at some point in the future. The goal of annuities is to provide a steady stream of income during retirement.

There are a lot of different types of annuities in the marketplace today. They offer various features and benefits that you can choose to fit your particular situation. For example, you can now lock in downside protection and still benefit from upside growth in the stock market. You can also lock in favorable interest rates. I strongly suggest that you set up a consultation with a professional financial advisor to help guide you during this important life stage. Please make sure the advisor you work with has experience working with retirees specifically.

Below is a list of the most common reasons that individuals and couples preparing for retirement consider purchasing annuities:

- Deferral of taxes is a big benefit.
- Large sums of money can be put into an annuity—more than is allowed annually in a 401(k) plan or an IRA—either all at once or over a period of time.
- Flexible payout options can help retirees meet their cash flow needs.
- Annuities offer a death benefit. Generally, if the contract owner or annuitant dies before the annuitization stage, the beneficiary will receive a death benefit at least equal to the net premiums paid.
- Annuities can help an estate avoid probate; beneficiaries receive the annuity proceeds without time delays and probate expenses.
- One of the most appealing benefits of an annuity is the option for a guaranteed lifetime income stream.
- When you purchase an annuity contract, your annuity assets will accumulate tax-deferred until you start taking withdrawals in retirement. Distributions of earnings are taxed as ordinary income. Withdrawals taken prior to age 59½ may be subject to a ten percent federal income tax penalty.

Fixed Annuities

Fixed annuities are annuity contracts with insurance companies that pay a fixed rate of return. If you start receiving income immediately, the annuity is called a SPIA, or Single Premium Immediate Annuity. You can also purchase a fixed annuity but postpone the income payments until a future date. This type of fixed annuity is called a *deferred annuity*. Although the rate on a fixed annuity may be adjusted, it will never fall below a guaranteed minimum rate specified in the annuity contract. This guaranteed rate acts as a floor to help protect owners from periods of low interest rates.

Variable Annuities

Variable annuities offer fluctuating investment returns. The owner of a variable annuity allocates premiums to investment subaccounts of their own choosing. These subaccounts can be invested in mutual funds, which range from very low risk to very high risk. The investment return on a variable annuity is based on the performance of the subaccounts selected. Variable annuity subaccounts fluctuate with changes in market conditions. When a variable annuity is surrendered, or "cashed in," the value of the annuity may be worth more or less than the original amount invested.

Variable annuities have been a bit controversial over the years. They are more complex products than simple, fixed annuities. There are different pros and cons to consider. Like medicine, variable annuities can be very beneficial for some retirees, but disastrous for others. I suggest educating yourself on the pros and cons of variable annuities so you can decide whether or not a variable annuity makes sense for your unique financial plan. Below is a list of some pros and cons so you can begin to understand the unique characteristics of variable annuities:

Variable Annuity Pros:

Variable annuity subaccounts are designed to imitate mutual funds, which allow investors to invest their money to grow and receive high rates of return.

- Many states protect the proceeds of insurance assets from lawsuits, which make variable annuities an attractive growth investment for business owners and professionals threatened with liability lawsuits.

- Many variable annuities have provisions that allow the owner to take annual cash withdrawals of up to ten percent of the principal investment. A waiver of surrender charges for various contingencies, ranging from disability to terminal illness, is also sometimes offered.

- There is no limitation on the amount invested inside a variable annuity. Contract holders do not face the annual contribution limits currently placed on holders of IRAs, 401(k)s, and other tax-advantaged retirement plans.

- IRA accounts require minimum required distributions to begin no later than when the account holder reaches age 70½. There is no such requirement for variable annuity distributions.

- A variable annuity holder can withdraw funds at their discretion once distribution commences or, alternatively, convert funds into a life annuity guaranteeing lifelong income.

- In the last decade or so, variable annuities have increasingly offered living benefit riders that guarantee levels of yield, income, and withdrawals. These have proved popular.

Variable Annuity Cons:

Perhaps the biggest restriction on variable annuities is that they are expensive from a fee standpoint. Variable annuity subaccounts incur expenses that detract from their annual yield, just like the mutual funds that they mimic. But the insurance company incurs additional expenses in operating the subaccounts and adding insurance features, such as death benefits and guarantees. Total annual expenses may reach three percent or more. Surrender charges and penalties for premature withdrawal threaten to add to the list of fees.

- Unlike mutual funds, variable annuities do not receive a step-up in cost basis to the valuation as of date of death, making them unattractive for estate-planning purposes. In most cases, when an asset is passed on to a beneficiary, its value is more than what it was when the original owner acquired it. The asset therefore receives a step-up in basis so that the beneficiary's capital gains tax is minimized. Variable annuities do not have this benefit.

- Variable annuities have surrender charges that often run as high as five to ten percent in the first two years after purchase, tapering off to one percent in succeeding years. The charges may last for as long as ten years or, rarely, longer. Premature withdrawals (made prior to the annuity holder reaching age 59½) incur a ten percent early withdrawal tax penalty as well as ordinary income taxes.

Don't Forget about Social Security Benefits

Many people assume that Social Security will not be available for them when they retire. There is a widespread fear that the government program will go bankrupt. The reality is this: No one knows for sure what the future holds. Every time we get a new president and/or government administration, the rules and policies regarding Social Security can change. For now, the program is in place and can provide a nice income stream during your retirement. *If you have paid a portion of your paycheck into Social Security for years, please do not overlook this valuable retirement benefit.* For new retirees, or those approaching age sixty-two, this benefit will most likely have a positive effect on your retirement plans.

Every individual and/or married couple in America has different financial needs and goals. As a result, the best time to start drawing Social Security benefits will vary greatly from person to person. It's a decision every individual must address by themselves or with their family. For example, many people are unaware that if they are currently divorced, but were married at least ten years to a Social Security-eligible beneficiary, and they are at least sixty-two years old, they may access a former spouse's earnings record. In addition, if your spouse was benefits-eligible for Social Security, but predeceased you, you may also be eligible to receive benefits from his or her Social Security. The first step is to contact the IRS at the following website: www.socialsecurity. gov/myaccount and ask for a current summary of your benefits as well as your spouse's benefits if applicable.

You will need the following information available in order to estimate your future Social Security benefits:

1. Current marital status (Single, Married, Divorced, Widowed)
2. Your date of birth and/or your spouse's date of birth
3. Whether or not you and/or your spouse worked for a government agency for at least ten years
4. Your average salary per year and/or your spouse's average salary per year.[2]

How much you have saved in cash, brokerage accounts, retirement accounts, and other assets and investments is the most important factor in deciding when to begin drawing your benefits. Obviously, the more assets you have on hand, the more options you will have in determining the best time to begin drawing your benefits. Full retirement age is now sixty-seven. However, you can start receiving partial benefits as early as age sixty-two. The longer you wait to start receiving your Social Security benefits, the greater your monthly income will be from Social Security. If each of us knew exactly how long we would live, then this would be an easy decision. When people ask me when they should start collecting their Social Security benefits, I always respond, "It depends." This is just another example of how a retirement plan from a qualified financial advisor would be very valuable. Do you see a theme here?

How Do I Withdraw Money to Live on during Retirement?

Another very important aspect of preparing for retirement involves how to best take out distributions from employer-sponsored retirement plans, such as a 401(k), upon retirement. Retirees are faced with a few broad options. Is it better to take the payout in the form of systematic payments, a lifetime annuity, or a lump sum? Let's discuss each strategy.

Systematic Withdrawals

Some retirement plans may allow you to take systematic withdrawals: either a fixed dollar amount on a regular schedule, a specific percentage of the account value on a regular schedule, or the total value of the account in equal distributions over a specified period of time.

The Lifetime Annuity Option

Your retirement plan may allow you to take payouts as a lifetime annuity, which converts your account balance into guaranteed monthly payments based on your life expectancy. If you live longer than expected, the payments continue anyway.

There are several advantages associated with this payout method. It helps you avoid the temptation to spend a significant amount of your assets at one time and the pressure to invest a large sum of money that might not last for the rest of your life. Also, there is no large initial tax bill on your entire nest egg; each monthly payment is taxed incrementally as ordinary income.

If you are married, you may have the option to elect a joint and survivor annuity. This would result in a lower monthly retirement payment than the single annuity option, but your spouse would continue to receive a portion of your retirement income after your death. If you do not elect an annuity with a survivor option, your monthly payments end upon your death.

The main disadvantage of the annuity option lies in the potential reduction of spending power over time. Annuity payments are not indexed for inflation. If we experienced a four percent annual inflation rate, the purchasing power of the fixed monthly payment would be halved in eighteen years.

Lump-Sum Distribution

If you elect to take the money from your employer-sponsored retirement plan as a single lump sum, you would receive the entire vested account balance in one payment, which you can invest and use as you see fit. You would retain control of the principal and could use it whenever and however you wish.

Of course, if you choose a lump sum, you will have to pay ordinary income taxes on the total amount of the distribution in one year. A large distribution could easily move you into a higher tax bracket. Another consideration is the twenty percent withholding rule: Employers issuing a check for a lump-sum distribution are required to withhold twenty percent toward federal income taxes. Thus, you would receive only eighty percent of your account balance, not one hundred percent. Distributions taken prior to age 59½ are also subject to a ten percent federal income tax penalty.

There is good news though. To avoid some of these tax issues, you can choose to roll the balance of the funds directly to an IRA in order to maintain the tax-deferred status of the funds. An IRA rollover might provide you with more options, not only in how you choose to invest the funds, but also in how you access the funds over time.

A personal financial advisor can help you determine the best way to not only invest your retirement funds, but also distribute those funds in a way that supports your lifestyle and protects your nest egg. Many people who have successfully managed their own investments up until now, often decide to consult with a financial advisor at this crucial stage in their life, when they are moving from accumulation of assets to their distribution.

Lessons for a Successful Transition to Retirement

Friend, I want you to understand that it really is possible to successfully transition from making money to spending money while in retirement, just like Bonnie did. Here are some lessons from her life.

- Have a realistic monthly budget established at the beginning of your retirement. I suggest using the budget worksheet I included at the end of chapter two. Modify the budget to include only income you will have during retirement. In addition, determine which expenses will decrease or be eliminated after you retire from working (i.e., dry cleaning, gas for commuting, lunches, etc.). Your budget will most likely look a lot different during your retirement years.

- Your goal should be to have no debt and own a home free and clear before you retire. Owning your own home without a mortgage significantly increases your financial security. It also decreases your cost of living during retirement. If you have a large home with a mortgage, you should definitely consider selling your large home and paying cash for a much less expensive home. Smaller homes are also easier to maintain both physically and financially.

- Determine if there is a gap between the income you will receive automatically from pensions and/or Social Security, and what you will need each month to cover your monthly expenses.

- If you have not already done so, consider hiring a personal financial advisor to evaluate your financial plans for retirement.

- If there is an additional monthly income need, consider purchasing an annuity that will provide another income stream for you during retirement.

- Make sure you have a conservative investment portfolio for the remainder of your liquid assets that can provide you with upside growth potential, but significant downside protection.
- Determine if you have enough assets to be self-insured, or if your estate could benefit from life insurance.
- If you retire prior to age sixty-five, you will need health insurance. You cannot enroll in Medicare until age sixty-five. Have a plan for how you will pay for your health insurance *before* you retire. A lot of people continue to work, at least part time, until age sixty-five in order to keep their health insurance through their employer.
- You should also budget for long-term care insurance premiums unless your assets are significant enough that you are self-insured.
- Make sure your will and estate plan are current and match your desires for your estate and your beneficiaries (see chapter ten).
- Consider creating a binder that contains all of your important financial documents. Then store the binder in a very secure place, such as a safe deposit box at a bank or a fireproof safe in your home. This will allow the executor of your estate to properly manage your affairs if something happens to you unexpectedly.

I hope Bonnie has inspired you to evaluate your current financial situation. It takes a lot of pressure off of you not to have to worry about it if you have a plan in place. *Please remember, focus on planning for living and not dying!*

Investing in the Kingdom of God during Retirement

I want to encourage you to invest your money, both before and after retirement. You have to decide which strategy or combination of strategies is right for your particular situation.

Friend, all of your money belongs to God. He wants you to use it wisely, grow it, and bless others with it. One final way you can do that is by investing in the kingdom of God, both before and after you retire from your career. How do you do that? Here are some examples:

- Contribute to your church or synagogue
- Fund a scholarship at your favorite college or university
- Support missionaries
- Fund a local charity
- Sponsor a child

The list of how to bless others is endless! So how do you choose where to invest your kingdom funds? Go back to chapter three for a discussion on how to prayerfully choose which causes to support.

I also want to empower you to think boldly and outside of the box about investing your most precious commodity, your time. Some people have more time than discretionary income to volunteer and support local ministries, churches, and non-profit organizations. This is especially true for many retirees. Volunteering to serve others and invest in kingdom causes is a great legacy to leave. Let's make sure we're being wise stewards of both our time and our money throughout our adult lives and into our retirement. The reality is that we will all be accountable one day for how we lived our lives. Second Corinthians 5:10 reminds us, "For we must all appear before the judgment seat of Christ, so that each of us may receive what is due us for the things done while in the body, whether good or bad." To conclude this chapter, I love what Corrie ten Boom famously said, "Life should never be measured by its duration but by its donation."

CHAPTER 9

My Kids Want to Go to College. Now What?

SECRET #9: THE FAITHFUL SAVE FOR COLLEGE

> *Instruct the wise and they will be wiser*
> *still;*
> *teach the righteous and they will add*
> *to their learning.*

Proverbs 9:9

I recently had the opportunity to visit with a group of twelve women to get their perspective on paying for college for their children. I asked each person if they had started saving for college for their children, and what they planned to provide, if possible, for their kids. I really liked what my friend Mary Annelle had to share. Interestingly enough, Mary Annelle was one of my college roommates at Texas A&M University. It seems very surreal that she and I are now discussing how we'll pay for college for our own children. The common thread among the women I interviewed is that they all value education and believe it's a gift. I couldn't agree more. *Secret number nine is to save for college now, so the cost of tuition and fees is not a burden to your family in the future.* This is a huge way for parents and grandparents to move from fearful insecurity to confident control, as it relates to their personal finances.

Mary Annelle and her husband, Bryan, have always been very purposeful with financial planning. Bryan is a lawyer and also has an MBA. He is quite analytical. Mary Annelle stays at home with their four children and does a great job managing her household budget and all of the responsibilities of caring for four children. As a couple, Mary Annelle and Bryan feel that it's their responsibility to pay for college for their four children. However, it is not, "Whatever they want, wherever they want to go." They are budgeting to pay for four years of tuition at a public, state school for each of their children. If any of their four children decide to attend an out-of-state or private university, they will have to supplement the cost of their education with student loans, scholarships, or income they generate themselves.

Mary Annelle and Bryan are already having discussions with their children about college. They want to let their kids know early in life what to expect from them financially as parents. There will be no surprises when their kids are old enough to start applying to college. Mary Annelle and Bryan have been saving for each child's education with 529 college savings plans. God willing, they'll be prepared financially to pay for the expenses of college for all four children, if they continue with the savings plans they have already established. Most important, they have not sacrificed their own retirement savings. They agree that it's not an option to consider using their retirement savings to supplement the cost of a private or out-of-state university.

Mary Annelle and Bryan have avoided a common mistake I often see people make. They choose to allocate all of their discretionary income toward college savings needs for their children, and then *not* save for retirement. For example, a family has kids in high school with plans to go off to college in just a few short years. Retirement, on the other hand, seems very far away. In reality, college students can get financial aid. They can also work while going to school, and help pay for some of their own expenses if necessary. *Parents cannot take out a loan for retirement.* Please don't misunderstand me. I'm *not* advocating that you not save for a college education for your child. However, I do want to emphasize that retirement savings has to be your first priority.

The best part about proactive financial planning for both college savings needs for your children and retirement, is that it takes any guessing and emotion out of the financial decisions that must be made over time. Everyone's expectations are managed early on. Mary Annelle and Bryan are great examples of being proactive, rather than reactive, with their financial decisions.

Ways to Save for College

Parents do well to plan ahead for college, as the cost can be prohibitive. According to the College Board, the average annual cost of tuition for the 2016–2017 school year was $33,480 at private colleges, $9,650 for state residents at public colleges, and $24,930 for out-of-state residents attending public universities. However, these figures do not include the cost of room and board, books, supplies, and transportation.[1]

The steady rise in the cost of a college education has slowed somewhat during the past two years. That's good news for families with current or future students. But even so, college is expensive. Despite the cost, higher education is still a valuable investment. In general, college graduates not only earn more than nongraduates, but also tend to be healthier, more satisfied with their jobs, and more likely to remain employed during tough economic times. A strategic savings plan is a key step toward providing your student with the many benefits of a college diploma. I agree with Benjamin Franklin, "An investment in knowledge pays the best interest."

Many parents wonder, *What is the best way to save for my child's college education?* I have good news for you. There are now more tax credits and savings vehicles specifically for college expenses than ever before. The best time to start saving for your children's college expenses is now. The earlier you start saving, the more likely your child will have the opportunity to attend college, without a large financial burden to either one of you.

As I mentioned previously, it's very important to find a balance between saving for college education costs for your children, while also continuing to save for your own retirement. Keep the following facts in mind when thinking about college savings needs for your children, while also saving for your own retirement years:

- Be sure to take advantage of any employer sponsored retirement plans such as a 401(k), or 403(b) tax-sheltered annuity. If your employer offers a match to any of your personal pre-tax retirement plan contributions, be sure to invest the maximum that your employer will match, *before* you allocate any more discretionary income to college savings accounts.
- Your IRA accounts *can* be used as secondary funding sources to help pay for college expenses for your children. You're allowed to take funds out of a traditional IRA or Roth IRA without paying the ten percent early withdrawal penalty, if the funds are used to pay for qualified education expenses. However, you should *not* use this option if you need these funds for your retirement.
- The only way to use funds in your 401(k) plan to help pay for college for your children is to take a loan, up to a maximum of $50,000. Unlike withdrawals from an IRA to pay for college expenses, any loan taken from a 401(k) plan must be paid back. I do *not* recommend this option; unless

you're certain that you have the cash flow available to pay the loan back to your 401(k) plan.

- Always remember that if you use some of your own retirement accounts to pay for your children's college expenses today, the funds might not be there for you when you need them in retirement. You risk paying for college for your kids now, only to be a burden to them later in life.

I want to teach you how to afford to pay for college for your children. It can be done. The first step is to do research to determine how much it could potentially cost to send your child to college. The website www.savingforcollege.com has lots of valuable resources for parents and students, in addition to a great college savings calculator. If you want to determine now approximately how much it will cost to send your child to college in the future, you'll be asked to enter the following variables in the online savings calculator:

- The age of your child
- How much you have already saved, if any
- What type of college or university you are willing to pay for, such as local community college, a state university, an out-of-state university, or a private university

The calculator will then estimate the future education costs for your child. Please remember, just like any other projection, the calculations are based on variables that may change over time.

There are multiple ways for your children to receive a college education. Try to keep an open mind when considering various options for educating them. One way to save a considerable amount of money on tuition, as well as other fees and expenses, is to have your child attend a local community college for the first two years of college. You'll save even more money if your child can continue to live at home while attending community college.

Then neither the child nor the parent will have to pay rent for an apartment or the cost of room and board in a dormitory.

Another idea to consider is an in-state public university in the state in which you currently live. Tuition and fees for public universities are considerably more affordable than private universities, or out-of-state public universities. You'll have to decide which type of school is best for your child and affordable for your family. I recommend going to visit some colleges and universities way before your child plans to actually attend college. The decision will be much less emotional, and together, you'll be more equipped to make a well-informed decision as a family.

Please ensure you don't overlook the opportunity for scholarships and grant money to offset the cost of your child's college expenses. If your child receives scholarship or grant money, they'll never have to pay that money back after graduation. It's well worth the effort to seek out and apply for federal grants and private scholarships. You have to do your research and go the extra mile and apply for as many scholarship programs as possible. Most universities offer both academic scholarships as well as athletic scholarships. In addition, there are organizations such as rotary clubs, women's service clubs, or the YMCA who give money away every year to kids headed off to college. There are also websites now that help aggregate different scholarship opportunities based on age, gender, race, area of study, SAT scores, grades, etc. Check out: https://scholarshipowl.com.

When I was headed off to Texas A&M University for undergraduate studies, I did lots of research and applied for many scholarships. I honestly spent more time applying for scholarships than I did to universities. My situation was a little unique. My dad was an Aggie, my great-grandfather was an Aggie, and my uncle was an Aggie. My husband is an Aggie too. I just didn't know him yet at that time. You get the idea. The Aggie brainwashing starts very early in my family, as well as many other Texas A&M alumni families. Usually the first Aggie shirt is given at the ripe old age of "birth," before leaving the hospital to go home. I'm already working on my own kids now. If kids think there's only one university mom and dad will pay for, that helps too! Sorry, I digressed a little there.

After I applied for many scholarships and went through a lot of interviews, I was awarded a rotary club scholarship that helped tremendously to offset the cost of my undergraduate education. It took a lot of extra effort, but it was well worth my time after I was awarded scholarship money. My parents were also quite grateful.

In certain cases, the only way a child will be able to attend college is through student loans. There is no shame in that; it's actually quite common. Let's discuss the pros and cons of different ways to save for your children's future college education costs.

529 Plans

A 529 plan is a state or college-sponsored program designed to help families save for future higher-education expenses. The funds in a 529 savings plan accumulate on a tax-deferred basis and can be withdrawn free of federal income tax when used for qualified education expenses at accredited post-secondary schools, such as colleges, universities, community colleges, and certain technical schools. Qualified expenses include tuition, fees, books, and supplies.

A common question is whether or not funds in a 529 plan can be used for the cost of room and board. The answer is, "yes and no." Room and board costs *in excess* of the amount the specific university reports in its "cost of attendance" figures for federal financial aid purposes may not be paid for with a 529 plan.

Two very beneficial features of 529 college savings plans are the following:

- The high contribution limits (set by each state)
- There are no income restrictions for donors.

The maximum amount that may be contributed on behalf of each designated beneficiary to a 529 plan varies among states and can change at any time. However, it is much higher than any other type of college savings plan. For example, in Texas you can contribute up to $452,210[2] without any income limit for the donor making the contributions. On the other hand, you can only contribute $2,000 annually to a Coverdell education savings account and the income limit to contribute is limited to individuals with a modified adjusted gross income (MAGI) less than $110,000, or $220,000 if filing a joint return.[3]

Each 529 plan has its own rules and restrictions, which can change at any time. As with other investments, there are generally fees and expenses associated with participation in a 529 savings plan. There is also the risk that the investments may lose money or not perform well enough to cover college costs as anticipated. The tax implications of a 529 plan should be discussed with a tax advisor because they can vary significantly from state to state. Most states offer their own 529 programs, which may provide advantages and benefits exclusively for their residents and taxpayers.

Most 529 plans offer a menu of investment options, so that you can tailor your investments to your child's age or to your own strategy. Owners of 529 plans are allowed to change their investment choices twice a year. Typically, if you invest in a fund that is tailored to your child's age, the 529 plan will adjust the account holdings as they age, investing more aggressively in stocks when they are young, and as they get close to college age, it will shift to a more conservative asset allocation that invests more heavily in bonds.

One drawback of 529 plans is that if your child ends up not attending college, you will have to pay taxes if you withdraw the money for any other use. However, you can always shift the beneficiary of the 529 plan to another immediate family member.

There are a few other investment vehicles that families are utilizing to save for college. It is always best if you understand the pros and cons of each option in order to make an informed decision about which plan is best for your family's future education needs.

Education Savings Account (ESA)

Like a 529 plan, an ESA is a tax-deferred savings account that allows your earnings and withdrawals to be free from federal income taxes, as long as the funds are used to pay for higher education expenses. One of the cons of an ESA is that there are income limitations on who is allowed to invest money in an ESA for their children. The minimum initial allowable investment ranges from $0 to $100,000. However, the maximum allowable annual contribution is only $2,000. That's why I prefer a 529 plan to an ESA.

Prepaid Tuition 529 plan

This is currently my favorite way to save for college expenses for my own children, as well as my client's children and/or grandchildren. This is the only product that allows you to lock in the future cost of state tuition in today's dollars. Since the annual cost of tuition and fees has historically way outpaced inflation, this will provide a substantial savings to a family that starts saving for college when their child is young.

You must purchase a prepaid 529 plan for the state in which you live, or the state in which you intend for your children to attend college. For example, I live in Texas so I have purchased the Texas version of this 529 plan called the Texas Tuition Promise Fund.

In a prepaid tuition plan, you purchase units that are equivalent to a certain number of semester hours. Fifty units in the

Texas Tuition Promise Fund will pay for fifteen hours of state tuition and fees. So one hundred units will pay for thirty semester hours, which is normally the full-time workload for one year of college. If your child doesn't attend an in-state university or community college, you will receive a transfer value of the units at the time they are needed to apply toward the tuition and fees, at either a private university or an out-of-state school.

Just like with a regular 529 plan, you may also change the beneficiary to another child or family member if the funds are not used. Another question I'm often asked is if you can transfer assets between different types of 529 plans. The answer is yes. For example, I have a client who lives in Texas and has funded a prepaid Texas Tuition Promise Fund 529 plan. His son is the beneficiary and is a senior in high school. His son was recently accepted to the University of Alabama and received a 75% scholarship. His parents will pay for the remaining 25% of his tuition, fees, room and board, etc. My client rolled the funds in the prepaid Texas 529 plan to a traditional 529 plan that's making a higher investment return because he no longer needs the prepaid tuition benefit for the state of Texas.

I believe it's a great conversation starter for parents to talk to their children now about what to expect financially from them in the future. I have a lot of clients that have purchased a prepaid tuition plan. If their child decides to go to an out-of-state college or private university, the child will have to get scholarships, grants, student loans, or work in order to supplement the additional cost of tuition and fees. This puts the decision back in the child's court, rather than the parent's court, as to where to attend college for the best bang for their buck.

Universal Life Insurance

Universal life insurance policies build cash value through regular premiums and grow at competitive rates. The policies carry a death benefit. In addition to providing cash to your heirs in the event of your death, money can be withdrawn from these contracts through policy loans, often at no interest. The withdrawals may reduce the policy's death benefit, but you are free to use the funds inside the policy however you wish. Some families are using life insurance for more than one financial goal. They are using some of the cash that grows tax-deferred to pay for college expenses for their children. The insurance policy protects their family in the event of death, but it also is a savings vehicle with tax advantages and protection from creditors and legal suits. This is a creative way to have your money work hard for you because it serves multiple purposes at the same time.

Mutual Funds

As you learned in the last chapter, an investment company establishes mutual funds by pooling the monies of many different investors and then investing that money in a diversified portfolio of securities. These securities are selected to meet the specific goals of the fund. The value of mutual fund shares fluctuates with market conditions so that, when sold, shares may be worth more or less than their original cost. The reason some families are choosing to use mutual funds invested in a taxable portfolio, rather than 529 college savings plans, is because there is more flexibility with how to use the funds in the future. Some families earmark their mutual funds for future college expenses, but they can also use them as a safety net if the family has an emergency or urgent liquidity need. The disadvantage of this route is that you will give up the tax advantage of growing your money in a 529 plan. The advantage of this route is that if your child ends up not going to college, you will not incur any tax penalty to withdraw this money for other uses.

Parameters for Student Performance

When I met with the women who were discussing the subject of saving for college for their children, one person mentioned putting parameters on their child's performance during college. Here is how this works: You have them sign a contract before they go to college if you are paying for their tuition. Therefore, there is open communication and there are no surprises. Some great parameters to consider for your own children are the following:

- Your child must maintain a 3.0 grade point average or higher for you to continue to pay for their tuition while they attend college.
- If your child fails a course, the child is responsible for paying the parents back for the tuition of the course they failed.
- The child must finish school in four years. They know when they start their freshmen year at college that you will not pay for more than four years of school. Obviously, if there are extenuating circumstances you can adjust this over time. However, manage your child's expectations *before* they start college so they don't falsely believe they're on an unlimited gravy train.
- Some parents will only pay for tuition, but not for room and board. This encourages a child to choose a local school so they can live at home and save considerable money on their living expenses.

If you decide you want to pay for your child's education, the best way to meet your future school savings needs is little by little over time. Proverbs 13:11 reminds us, "Dishonest money dwindles away, but whoever gathers money little by little makes it grow." I encourage you to do your research and come up with a realistic budget for the cost of educating your children. Use the online calculator I mentioned previously at www.savingforcollege.com

to determine how much you need to start saving today to meet your future goals.

Other Routes to Success

As much as I believe in education, I also understand that a four-year bachelor's degree is not for everyone. One of the worst ways to waste money would be to send a child to college who has no interest in being there, or has not demonstrated the ability to handle it. Don't worry; there are other routes to a viable career. Your money might be better spent sending your child to a trade school. Some 529 plans have provisions that allow the funds to be used to pay for vocational schools. You will need to verify this with your particular plan.

Some students might benefit from the discipline and structure of the military. This plan will allow them time to mature and also earn tuition assistance credits for their service. The Post-9/11 GI Bill became effective on August 1, 2009, and has the most comprehensive education benefits package since the original GI Bill was signed into law in 1944. Most important, do your research so you know what options are available for your children and/or grandchildren.

I strongly believe that education is a valuable gift to give to your children and/or grandchildren. Education is a legacy, and it's one of the greatest equalizers in our society. It teaches an individual to think and to analyze. It's a means to freedom and independence rather than dependence. Maimonides, a Spanish philosopher born in 1135, is famous for teaching the following: "Give a man a fish and you feed him for a day; teach a man to fish and you feed him for a lifetime." Isn't it interesting that nothing has changed in almost a thousand years?

CHAPTER 10

Proper Estate Planning
Is a Great Legacy

*Whatever you do, work at it with all your heart, as
working for the Lord, not for human masters, since
you know that you will receive an inheritance from the
Lord as a reward. It is the Lord Christ you are serving.*

Colossians 3:23–24

My friend Elizabeth has experienced the death of two close
family members in the last couple of years. It has been a
tough time of grieving and change for her and her family.

She learned firsthand during her grieving process what an
incredible gift it is to the survivors, if the deceased family member
had a well-thought-out estate plan and a current will. Elizabeth's
sister is now a widow with two young children. She has been
able to take time to grieve because her husband had plenty of life
insurance to support her and her small children. As a result, she
was not forced to go back to work immediately upon her husband's death. She was a stay-at-home mom before her husband
died. Since she received adequate life insurance proceeds, she has
continued to be a stay-at-home mom. The life insurance proceeds

have allowed her to create as much of a sense of normalcy as possible for her children while they were grieving as well.

Please don't misunderstand. Money never replaces a loved one. However, if someone is going to die and leave a widow behind, it's a much better situation if she is not also financially devastated at the exact same time that she's grieving and figuring out how to move forward with her life.

Sadly, Elizabeth's mother-in-law *also* passed away recently. She was in her eighties and had lived a long and fruitful life. She was the proud mother of seven sons and seven daughters-in-law, as well as numerous grandchildren. That's a lot of family members that could have various opinions on how her estate should have been divided up financially. This didn't happen in Elizabeth's family, but sometimes money can drive a wedge between family members who have never had any issues before.

Her mother-in-law had her affairs perfectly organized. She even left handwritten notes to her son who was the executor of the estate with instructions for closing bank accounts, credit cards, and even magazine subscriptions, immediately upon her death. Everything was in a binder with an up-to-date will, all investment and bank account information, and her specific desires for family heirlooms. There was absolutely no margin for misunderstanding among any of her heirs. Elizabeth has witnessed what a gift proper estate planning is to the surviving family members and the executor of the estate, which happened to be her husband. It has inspired her and her husband to make sure their financial affairs are well thought out and organized, so their children will not have to worry about anything besides grieving at their deaths.

The Importance of a Will

Why is it so important to have a will? It allows you to have sole discretion over the distribution of your assets. You get to decide how your belongings, such as jewelry or family heirlooms, should be distributed when you die. If you have a business or real estate investments, a will also determines who will be the beneficiary of those assets.

If you have minor children, the most important reason to have a will is that it allows you to appoint a guardian, whom you know and trust, to care for them if you pass away. If you have children from a prior marriage, even if they are adults, your will can dictate the assets they receive. Having your wishes and desires spelled out specifically in a will also minimizes tensions between survivors. If you're charitably inclined, a will also allows you to gift a predetermined amount, or percentage of your assets, to the charity of your choice upon your death.

You should also be aware of what a will *cannot* do. Wills normally address the distribution of the majority of your assets, but there are a variety of items that are not covered by the instructions in a will. Such items include:

- Community property
- Proceeds from life insurance policy payouts
- Retirement assets
- Assets owned as joint tenants with rights of survivorship
- Investment accounts that are designated as "transfer on death"

Do you have a current will? If you do have a will, was it originally written and notarized in the state in which you now live? This is one of the biggest mistakes that I encounter when consulting potential clients. They are unaware that if they have moved since they prepared a will, it's no longer applicable in the new state in which they currently live.

It's very important to make certain that the people you name as beneficiaries of your life insurance policies and retirement plans are correct and up-to-date. I recommend that you review your beneficiary designations for accuracy every two to three years. This is a very expensive mistake that you don't want to make. People often forget whom they originally listed on their life insurance policies, annuities, or retirement accounts as beneficiaries. Life happens. People divorce and/or remarry. Things change.

The worst illustration I have encountered from a financial planning perspective occurred when a gentleman died with a current will, but his life insurance beneficiaries had not been updated in over twenty years. He mistakenly left his life insurance proceeds to an ex-wife rather than his current wife. *That* is a big oops.

If you do *not* have a will when you pass away, you die "intestate," which means that the state government will oversee the distribution of your assets. Contrary to popular belief, the state does not inherit your assets. However, it will distribute your assets according to a set formula. The formula often results in half of your estate going to your spouse and the other half going to your children. This scenario can result in the sale of the family home, or other assets, which will negatively impact a surviving spouse.

Not having a will can create major financial and emotional difficulties, particularly if your spouse was counting on the bulk of your assets to maintain his or her standard of living. The biggest concern with not having a will arises if your children are minors. The court will appoint a representative to look after your children and their interests. Believe it or not, the number one reason that couples often avoid getting a will is that they cannot agree on a guardian for their children. Rather than coming to a decision, they procrastinate and do not get a will. This is a real travesty if both parents ever die in a common accident, without making proper preparations and plans to take care of their children.

Another common reason people don't get a will is that they're trying to save money. They will tell me, "It's not in the budget right now." I'm the biggest proponent you will ever meet about keeping a close eye on your monthly budget. However, if you die without a will, your lack of preparation will actually cost your heirs a lot of money, time, and heartache, especially if there are disagreements among family members about how your estate should be handled after your death. Wills no longer have to be prepared exclusively by an attorney. You can now get a will by using online software that allows you to customize a legal template to your particular situation. Then you can print the will after it's created on your own computer, and simply take it to a bank to have it notarized. You can now get a simple will at www.legaldocs.com or www.legalzoom.com for less than forty dollars. There really is no excuse for not getting a will.

Tax considerations are another very important issue to consider in order to preserve wealth when preparing your will. Proper estate planning and a well-designed will can minimize the tax liability of an individual's estate. Have you ever wondered what the estate tax is and how it may apply to you and your family?

The estate tax is a tax on your assets and property before they transfer to your beneficiaries upon your death. The reality is that most estates will *not* be subject to estate taxes. The estate tax may be repealed in the near future, but as of early 2017, only estates valued at more than $5.49 million (or $10.98 million for some married couples) would be subject to the federal estate tax. If, upon your death, the total value of your estate is less than the applicable exemption amount, no federal estate taxes will be due. If you have a substantial estate, please check with your tax advisor now, rather than later, to ensure that it's protected as much as possible from estate taxes upon your death, unless the IRS is your favorite charity. Then you don't have to worry. (I'm kidding!)

The most common exception to the federal estate tax is the unlimited marital deduction. The government exempts all transfers of wealth between a husband and wife from federal estate and gift taxes, regardless of the size of the estate. (The surviving spouse must be a US citizen to qualify for this exemption.) However, when the surviving spouse dies, the estate is subject to estate taxes, and only the surviving spouse's applicable exemption can be used.

Taxes are an important consideration in distributing your estate because the money your estate pays in taxes will not be available to your heirs. Each estate is allowed a federal estate tax exemption, which is an amount that can pass transfer-tax-free, either through lifetime gifts or upon death.

Estate Planning Documents

I want to encourage you to take time to get your estate planning documents in order. Below is a list of items you should address in order to leave your heirs the gift of an organized estate. I personally take this type of planning one step further with my clients. We create a binder and include a copy of all of the following documents in the binder. I call it: *The House Is On Fire Binder.* What that really means is that every document that is extremely important is in one place. If there is ever an emergency, you or your loved ones can grab the binder and have everything you need in one place to make important, and often life-changing, decisions.

Basic Will

A will is the most basic estate-planning document. It outlines who gets your stuff when you die (otherwise the state decides, and it's not always your spouse and/or kids) and who takes care of your minor children (otherwise a judge decides). A will also contains the name of your executor, who will administer your estate. Make sure he or she has a copy of your will and other pertinent documents.

Beneficiary Forms

Many people are surprised to learn that the beneficiary forms for life insurance policies and retirement accounts, that are filled out when a life insurance policy is applied for or a retirement account is opened, ultimately determine who gets the payouts when you die. *Your will does not determine who gets these payouts.* Friend, please make sure your beneficiary forms are up-to-date, and keep copies. As I mentioned previously, this is the most common mistake people make in estate planning. They have a current will, which is wonderful, but they forget to ensure that their other assets' beneficiary designations are correct as well.

Another mistake I often see when reviewing beneficiary forms occurs when minor children are listed as contingent beneficiaries on retirement accounts and/or life insurance policies. The well-meaning parents' plan was for assets to go to their children if the primary beneficiary, usually the surviving spouse, dies as well. The problem with this strategy is that you cannot leave money to minor children. Legally, an inheritance has to be left to minor children in a trust for their benefit so a trustee can manage it. This is another reason why consultations with professional estate-planning attorneys are very helpful.

Power of Attorney: Financial

By signing a durable power of attorney, you immediately give another person (your agent) the power to make financial and legal decisions on your behalf. The form can be customized so the agent has more or less power to do things like make annual exclusion gifts or change beneficiary designations on your retirement accounts.

Power of Attorney: Health Care

A health care power of attorney (or health care proxy) authorizes someone (your agent) to make medical decisions for you if you are unable to do so. Please be sure it includes a HIPPA provision, allowing your agent to access your medical information under HIPPA rules.

Living Will

In a living will, also known as an advanced medical directive, you indicate your end-of-life desires regarding prolonging medical care. If you have a chronic illness, consider tailoring it to your specific condition. Also, include an explanation of how to reconcile your choices with any family religious beliefs, if they conflict, to avoid any family discord.

Inventory of Investment Assets

Create a list of all bank accounts, savings accounts, and investment accounts. Be sure to include the account numbers and contact information for the companies servicing your accounts. Copies of statements for each account should definitely be included in your binder that we discussed previously.

List of Contacts

It's a very good idea to include a list of personal advisors to be included with your will and other estate planning documents. Include contact information for lawyers, bankers, financial planners, and tax advisors. In addition, if you own a home, consider making a list of utility and service providers (i.e., lawn care, pest control, magazine subscriptions). Your executor—and your heirs—will thank you.

Guide to Digital Assets

Make a list of your passwords for everything from your credit card accounts to your email accounts. One option is to utilize an online password storage service like www.keepass.com. Then you only have one password to remember. Give your executor and agent (under your power of attorney) instructions on how to find your password cheat sheet if needed in the future.

Funeral Arrangements

Consider adding a provision in your will stating your desires. If you clearly state your preference to either be cremated or buried, and where, it will take a lot of pressure off of your loved ones when they are grieving and making decisions regarding your funeral arrangements. A separate letter to your heirs in your own handwriting can include details and special wishes. If the letter is handwritten, it is more likely that your wishes will be carried out as you hoped.

Some people take planning for their funeral a step further and even buy burial insurance, which allows a person to prepay for their funeral. The purpose of this type of insurance is to ensure future funeral costs are not a burden on your loved ones after you pass away. Honestly, as long as you have at least $10,000 in liquid assets to cover the cost of a funeral, I would not purchase burial insurance.

Trusts

As I mentioned previously, if you have minor children (under age eighteen), please be sure your will creates a trust (and names a trustee) for any money left to them. Usually, the trustee is not the same person as the executor of your estate. This provides an extra check and balance.

Married couples may want to include a bypass, or disclaimer trust, created on the first spouse's death to preserve his or her estate tax exemption, or to protect the money from going to creditors, and/or a new spouse. The surviving spouse will then have access to the trust's earnings and principal, but what's left in the trust "bypasses" the survivor's estate. Other trusts to consider, that a licensed estate planning attorney can create for you, include: irrevocable life insurance trusts, qualified personal residence trusts, grantor-retained annuity trusts, and charitable trusts.[1]

Estate planning is typically the most dreaded aspect of personal financial planning, but it's also one of the most critical aspects of getting your financial affairs in order. Just like there never seems to be a perfect time to have a baby, there will never be a *perfect* time to begin the process of estate planning. If you're single, married with no kids, and/or have a very simple estate, my best advice is to use one of the online resources I mentioned previously to create the required documents. It will be the fastest and least expensive way to go.

However, if you have complicated family matters, own a business, and/or have significant assets, your best bet is to hire a certified estate-planning attorney that you either know, or has been referred to you by a trusted source. Call today and make an appointment to get the process started if you have not already done so. Then you can check this "to do" off your list and not think about it again. The only exception to this rule is if your circumstances in life change drastically such as marriage, divorce, or the birth of a child. Anytime you experience a major change in your life, re-evaluate your will and estate planning documents to make sure they are still relevant and appropriate for your current situation.

Having your estate and affairs in order provides peace of mind. It allows you to be confident, rather than fearful, that your family and heirs will be taken care of properly after you have passed away. Isn't that what every parent and grandparent wants for their family? *If you haven't started getting your estate and affairs in order, now is the time!*

God Will Provide

> *He provides food for those who fear*
> *him;*
> *he remembers his covenant forever.*

Psalm 111:5

My husband and I had the opportunity to travel to Israel as part of our spiritual journey in 2009. We fell in love with Israel and marveled at the opportunity to see the Bible come alive before our very eyes. We truly realized, then, that the stories in the Bible are not fictional. As a Christian, it's impossible to understand the heritage of your own faith if you do not understand the history and culture of the Jewish faith. I am a Judeo-Christian, as are you, if you believe in Jesus Christ as your Lord and Savior.

In order to begin the Holy Week prior to Easter this past year, I attended a Seder dinner, which is the traditional Jewish Passover meal. Toward the end of the Passover meal, the leader who is acting as the priest in a Jewish home, will begin to quote and sing the word *dayenu* ("die-yay-new"). *Dayenu* means that each act of God would have been enough, and for that alone we should be grateful. For each of his acts of mercy and kindness, we declare, "Dayenu."

During the Passover meal, each of the following statements is read aloud and we all say in unison, "Dayenu."

> LEADER: Had God brought us out of Egypt and not divided the sea for us.
>
> PEOPLE: Dayenu.
>
> LEADER: Had God divided the sea for us and not sustained us for forty years in the desert.
>
> PEOPLE: Dayenu.
>
> LEADER: Had God sustained us for forty years in the desert and not given us manna.
>
> PEOPLE: Dayenu.
>
> LEADER: Had God given us the Sabbath and not given us the Torah at Mount Sinai.
>
> PEOPLE: Dayenu.
>
> LEADER: Had God given us the Torah at Mount Sinai and not led us into the land of Israel.
>
> PEOPLE: Dayenu.
>
> LEADER: How many and miraculous are the great deeds that our God has performed for us, from taking us out of Egypt to giving us the land of Israel.
>
> PEOPLE: Blessed are you, O God, for as you supplied the needs of our ancestors, so do you continue to provide for our needs today.

Beloved, nothing has changed. The God of Israel that provided manna for the Israelites in the desert is the same God today. He is still providing for the needs of each and every one of us. How he provides looks a little different in our modern culture, and will differ with each person, but the principles are the same.

My friend, Yvette Livesay-Wright, can testify to God's caring provision. Yvette and her husband, Michael, own a graphic design company. Michael is a very gifted artist and graphic designer. Yvette is very organized, analytical, and an astute businesswoman.

They are a great team because their skill sets complement one another very well. Together, they have learned firsthand what it looks like to count their blessings and be completely surrendered to God to provide for their needs.

After many years of praying and waiting for God to reveal his financial plan for them, Michael finally left the security of his full-time job to start their own graphic design business in 2011. The first couple of years in particular were very tough financially. Yvette grew more in her faith journey during that season than almost any other time in her life. Yvette is extremely bright, capable, and talented, certainly not a damsel in distress. For her, it was very unsettling to not have financial security. She could not control her destiny just by working harder. Instead, she learned dependency on God.

Yvette was kind enough to share her journal with me from the first lean years of their business. She calls it her *Daily Bread Report*. It is her modern-day version of *Dayenu*, which we now know means that each act of God would have been enough, and for that alone we should be grateful. For each of his acts of mercy and kindness, she learned to declare, "Dayenu."

Finances are tough as a new business owner. Michael and Yvette soon learned their clients were not aware of the urgency to pay their bills, even after work had already been completed and invoiced. This attitude was something that they couldn't control, and it meant they didn't have a steady paycheck coming in on a regular basis. Together, they chose to trust God no matter what. Yvette kept a record of God's faithfulness in their lives through a *Daily Bread Report*. She wrote down the dollar amount, to the penny, that they needed each day to pay a certain bill in black. Then she recorded in red on the day that God provided for that particular need and exactly how much he provided. Honestly, when I looked at her journal, I was completely astounded to see all of the red ink, recording how God met their needs one step at a time, over and over again. The numbers could not lie.

The following is Yvette's personal testimony:

Every time God answered a specific prayer, I wrote it in red so that I couldn't miss it. There was a lot of red on the page! Looking at it now, I can see that for the most part, God only gave us what we needed, and not much more. Honestly, I appreciate that because it solidified in my mind that God was clearly at work. If you review the report, the amount God blessed us with each time almost matched exactly what the need was. The numbers are so close that I could never mistake God's gifts as a coincidence. The report also reminded me on a daily basis that God gives me everything I need daily . . . just enough for today, like manna for the Israelites.

Interestingly, during July and August of 2011, God did not provide according to what I asked for. I knew God was still at work, trying to teach me something. The months before, when he provided so perfectly for our needs, prepared me for this season. A friend wisely brought to my attention the story of Shadrach, Meshach, and Abednego while we were anxiously draining our savings account because no funds were arriving in our mailbox to pay our bills.

Shadrach, Meshach, and Abednego were three young men from Jerusalem, condemned to death in a fiery furnace by Nebuchadnezzar, king of Babylon, when they refused to bow down to an image of him and worship any god but the God of Israel. In fact, they even declared to the king, "If we are thrown into the blazing furnace, the God we serve is able to deliver us from it, and he will deliver us from Your Majesty's hand. But even if he does not, we want you to know, Your Majesty, that we will not serve your gods or worship the image of gold you have set up" (Dan. 3:17–18). An angry King Nebuchadnezzar then threw them into the flames, but God delivered them. And the astonished king declared, "Praise be to the God of Shadrach, Meshach and Abednego, who has sent his angel and rescued his servants! They trusted in him and defied the king's command and were willing to give up their lives rather than serve or worship any god except their own God" (Dan. 3:28).

Yvette told me how much the story of Shadrach, Meshach, and Abednego really resonated with her. She says that she has never forgotten it. "When we first started our business, I knew that God was able to bring the money in, but even if he didn't, he was still my God and I would still worship him." And that was the faith commitment that she was able to test in the lean months of 2011.

Take a moment to remember the ways that God has provided for your needs and, most likely, many of your wants throughout your life. It's very encouraging to look back and see all of the many ways that God has blessed us and watched over us, even when the circumstances were the toughest. You may want to start a *Daily Bread Report* just like my friend Yvette. Then you will also have a written testimony of God's faithfulness in your life. Remember, you can take heart that our God is fully sovereign and in control of the universe. You can trust him!

In Ephesians, Paul writes, "I pray that the eyes of your heart may be enlightened in order that you may know the hope to which he has called you, the riches of his glorious inheritance in his holy people" (Eph. 1:18).

This is my prayer for you: *that the eyes of your heart may be enlightened.* I hope you will pray about the financial topics discussed in this book. Then determine which positive steps forward you need to take today. Friend, the choice is yours. Will you live in fear about your finances? Or will you choose to have faith in the God who provides, and ask for his wisdom to be proactive with personal financial planning for you and your loved ones?

I encourage you to seek wise counsel and develop a financial plan for your future so you have direction. Every one of us needs a road map in life so we know where we're headed. Life will happen, and you will have to adjust your financial plan accordingly. Remember to be flexible.

Your first goal should be to make sure you have a cash reserve. Then assess your savings goals and needs, such as retirement and/or college planning, if you have not already done so. Start a realistic savings plan to meet your goals and commit to honor it every month. Take inventory of your spending habits. Do you have credit card debt that needs to be eliminated so you will not be enslaved to the lender? Maybe you're still trying to fill your heart with objects of this world instead of God's love for you.

One of the practical aspects of financial planning we discussed in this book is the need for insurance. Do you have life insurance and a current will in order to make sure that your children and/or spouse are taken care of in the event of your death? Is your ability to generate an income insured with a disability income insurance policy? Remember, while you're still healthy and able to go to work, your biggest financial asset is your ability to work and create wealth. Have you determined whether or not you or your parents need long-term care insurance to cover the cost of any unforeseen medical care in the future?

Are you currently giving to your church and to others that are in need? We live in the richest country in the world. However, there's still suffering and unmet needs all around us. Please, please know that work is honorable and noble. It allows us to provide for our families. However, your family's needs are not the only needs in the world. Providing for your family is your first priority and then beyond that, there's a whole world of need out there.

Friend, do not feel guilty about making money. If you allow guilt to motivate you, then you will sabotage your own success by letting your subconscious tell you that you're doing something wrong because you're making money. The Bible does not say that *money* is the root of evil. Rather, it is the *love* of money that is a root of all kinds of evil (1 Tim. 6:10). Money can be misused, but it's not the problem. The problem is actually a heart issue. This is an issue to be worked out between you and God. Be honest with yourself. Answer the following questions:

- What am I doing with my money?
- Am I being a wise steward, or investor, of the assets that God has given me?

In our world today, there is a false association between wealth and greed. Some of the poorest people in the world may be the greediest people you will ever meet. Some of the wealthiest people in the world may be the most generous. These facts may sound politically incorrect or controversial. However, greedy people covet what other people have, but they are not willing to work for money. Wealth comes with responsibility. It has the potential to change the trajectory of the future for yourself, your family, as well as other people and charities that you give to.

What are you really passionate about? Educating people? Providing access to clean water for those who don't have it? Spreading the gospel of Jesus Christ? The money you give away generously and strategically to nonprofit ministries in this world can have a ripple effect on bettering our world and furthering the kingdom of God.

Accumulating money is not something to feel guilty about; it's an honorable thing. Giving of your time by volunteering is noble. However, your time is a finite resource. You might have far more of an impact in this world if you use your time and gifts to generate money in order to support those already working in the mission field. They may be far better equipped to run their nonprofit organization than you are. Remember, we discussed the roles of kings and priests in chapter three. Prayerfully ask God to reveal to you what your specific role is in his kingdom. We're all an important part of the body of Christ.

Friend, the same God that brought the Israelites out of Egypt is the same God that we worship today. He wants to bless you. He wants a relationship with you. He will provide for your needs. But most of all, he wants your heart.

I'm so excited to see where this new journey to financial freedom takes you. I pray that you will take a moment to assess your personal financial affairs to determine what changes you need to make today, to move you from fearful insecurity to confident control. I also pray that you and your family will be blessed richly, both in this life and eternally as well. If you have accepted Jesus Christ as your personal Lord and Savior, then your life really is insured. I pray that you spend eternity with our very good God. As they say in the military right before they embark on an important mission, see you on the flipside!

Epilogue

By trade, I'm a financial advisor and author. By God's grace, I'm a wife and mother to two amazing kids. *Faithful Finance* is a book about ten secrets to living your best financial life possible. This epilogue is a list of ten secrets for living life well that God placed on my heart to share with my children. *Godspeed, little ones.*

10 Secrets for Living Life Well

1. Get an education. Do not settle. Go all the way. No one can ever take the gift of an education away from you. It's your key to opening many doors in life.
2. Read as many books as you can get your hands on. A well-read person is far more interesting and a much better communicator.
3. Exercise, preferably outdoors so you can also get some fresh air. You need to get your blood flowing to your brain every day for optimal performance, both mentally and emotionally.
4. Develop close friendships. Focus on quality of friendships, not quantity. You will need true friends to do life with. If a friend is not emotionally available to both celebrate your victories and cry during your disappointments, find a new friend.
5. Find a spouse who is supportive. No one in your life will ever make you happier or more miserable. Choose who you date both cautiously and wisely. Remember, you will never marry anyone whom you did not date first.
6. Develop relationships with mentors. Be humble and ask for advice. Seek out godly people a few stages ahead

of you in life that you both admire and respect. The majority of people will be very flattered if you ask them for their opinions and advice.

7. Be your sibling's best friend and biggest cheerleader. When your dad and I are gone, they will be the only person who will share *all* of your childhood memories. You will need each other. Love one another fiercely. (One more important thing: Be nice to your sibling's future wife or husband. If you're not friends with her or him, your sibling will become quite distant from you.)

8. You cannot be everything to everyone. Just focus on being the best *you* possible. Remember, I did not say you have to be the *best* . . . I said to strive to be the best version of *you*.

9. Do not focus on getting a job. You will never be passionate about it. Look for a *career*, which is a long-term lifestyle that supports your unique gift set and passions.

10. Most importantly: *Love God. Seek him.* He will always meet you exactly where you are. He has great plans in store specifically for you. Take time to pray and talk to him long enough to hear what he has to say.

∾

"For I know the plans I have for you," declares the Lord, "plans to prosper you and not to harm you, plans to give you hope and a future."

Jeremiah 29:11

Recommended Resources

http://makelemonade.co This website finds you the lowest rates on your student loans, credit cards, personal loans, banking, investments, and more.

www.emilystroud.net This is my personal website for Stroud Financial Management, Inc.

www.emilygstroud.com Enter your email address when prompted, and I will send you a free budget worksheet.

https://christianpf.com SeedTime website.

www.savingforcollege.com Great resource for questions regarding education savings plans and uses.

http://todaysmilitary.com/living/paying-for-college The military offers many educational benefits that service members can take advantage of during or after service.

www.irs.gov Official website for the IRS that you can utilize for questions regarding income tax issues.

www.charitynavigator.org Online resource that provides ratings and research regarding different nonprofit organizations.

www.legaldocs.com Website with resources if you are in need of a common legal document, like a contract to sell your car, a will, or an employment agreement.

https://scholarshipowl.com Website used to aggregate different scholarship opportunities based on age, gender, race, area of study, SAT scores, grades, etc.

www.keepass.com An online password storage service so you only have one password to remember.

www.mint.com Website used to create and monitor your monthly budget online.

Notes

Chapter 1: Let a Professional Worry

1. https://www.cfainstitute.org/programs/cfaprogram/
   Documents/1963_current_candidate_exam_results.pdf

Chapter 3: God is a Good Gift Giver

1. Rick Warren, "8 Reasons Believers Give to Your Church,"
   Pastors.com (October 24, 2013), http://pastors.com/8-reasons
   -believers-give-to-your-church
2. David R. High, *Kings and Priests* (Oklahoma City, Okla.: Books for
   Children of the World, 1993), 7.

Chapter 4: Do Not Borrow

1. https://well.blogs.nytimes.com/2007/11/23/when-shopping-puts
   -the-happy-in-your-holidays/
2. https://www.nerdwallet.com/blog/loans/compare-costs-buying
   -new-car-vs-used/
3. http://www.freddiemac.com/pmms/pmms30.htm

Chapter 5: Pay Yourself First

1. http://www.creditcards.com/credit-card-news/credit-card
   -industry-facts-personal-debt-statistics-1276.php
2. http://www.kait8.com/story/33829233/creditcardscom-weekly
   -credit-card-rate-report-average-card-apr-remains-at-1518
   -percent-for-eighth-week

Chapter 6: Is Your Life Insured?

1. https://www.census.gov/newsroom/releases/archives/
   miscellaneous/cb12-134.html
2. https://www.thebalance.com/short-term-disability-basics-1177839

Chapter 8: When Can I Transition

1. https://www.lendingclub.com/public/financial-advisor-overview
   .action
2. http://socialsecurityretire.org/how-to-use-the-social-security
   -retirement-calculator/

Chapter 9: My Kids Want to Go to College

1. http://www.collegedata.com/cs/content/content_payarticle_tmpl
   .jhtml?articleId=10064
2. http://money.usnews.com/529s/texas
3. https://www.irs.gov/publications/p970/ch07.html

Chapter 10: Proper Estate Planning

1. http://www.forbes.com/pictures/mjh45imjf/basic-will/

Special thanks to the *Faithful Finance* Launch Team

Noelle Ammerman

Timothy Determan

Amy Doze

Rebecca Dworaczyk

Carol Graham

Frank Graham

King Hoover

Donna Hopkins

Kim Hughes

Nate Johnson

Tamara Johnson

Kim Jones

LaCourdia Jones

Whitney Jones

Jenna Lee

Yvette Livesay-Wright

Cherie Lowe

Jennifer McAlister

Carmen Mota

Beth Penning

Patti Pierce

Julia Sable

Janna Taylor

Melissa Trimble

Melissa Moloney Walk

Sarah Webb

Angela Wells

Tamara Willmann

Social Media Director: Hayley Rodriguez

When Life Happens

We all have events that occur which not only affect our personal lives but our financial security as well. Whether you're taking a second look at your portfolio or just planning ahead, here are some circumstances that could influence your financial planning:

- Marriage or remarriage
- Divorce
- Birth or adoption of a child
- Purchase or sale of a home
- Job change
- Reduction in medical benefits
- A natural disaster
- Death of a close family member
- Major illness
- Long-term care of parents
- Paying off a major loan (home, business, college debt)
- Approaching or postponing retirement
- New or revised financial goals

If you have experienced any of these or other life changes this past year, you may benefit from making adjustments to your retirement plan, your budge,t or your portfolio. We can add security to your finances, regardless of what life brings your way.

Call to schedule a consultation
(866) 484-7019
www.emilystroud.net

Stroud
Financial Management, Inc.